proclamation 2

Aids for Interpreting the
Lessons of the Church Year

pentecost 1

**Leander E. Keck
and
Francis Wellford Hobbie**

series b

editors: Elizabeth Achtemeier · Gerhard Krodel · Charles P. Price

FORTRESS PRESS   PHILADELPHIA

Library of Congress Cataloging in Publication Data (Revised)

Main entry under title:

Proclamation 2.

    Consists of 24 volumes in 3 series designated A, B, and C which correspond to the cycles of the three year lectionary plus 4 volumes covering the lesser festivals. Each series contains 8 basic volumes with the following titles: Advent-Christmas, Epiphany, Lent, Holy Week, Easter, Pentecost 1, Pentecost 2, and Pentecost 3.
    CONTENTS: [etc.]—Series C: [1] Fuller, R. H. Advent-Christmas. [2] Pervo, R. I. and Carl III, W. J. Epiphany.—Thulin, R. L. et al. The lesser festivals. 4 v.
    1. Bible—Homiletical use. 2. Bible—Liturgical lessons, English.
[BS534.5.P76]   251   79–7377
ISBN 0–8006–4079–9 (ser. C, v. 1)

9415J81   Printed in the United States of America   1–4089

Contents

Editor's Foreword

Pentecost is the longest season of the church year, spanning twenty-eight Sundays in this series. As such, its lessons set forth what it means to be the church, the people of the New Covenant, the body of Christ. But its lessons do more than that. They mediate to us the power that enables us to grow up into Christian maturity, into the measure of the fullness of the stature of Christ. Such growth is a constant struggle, and the lessons of this season powerfully motivate and foster that growth.

On Pentecost and Trinity Sundays the mediation of the life-giving Spirit to the church is recalled and is to be reexperienced. We have been born anew in our baptisms, we are told, and we have been given the Spirit of sonship and of freedom, as heirs of God's promises. Further, each of us is given our own particular gift from the Spirit.

In the Sundays that follow, unfailing vitality and reassurance are offered us. We hear that we are set apart for God's purposes and not for humanity's, that our role is to be obedient to God in the power of the Spirit, and that the Spirit given us is a down payment of his coming kingdom. We are told that God in Christ is working a new creation in our lives over against all the chaos threatening them, that his mercy and healing are sure, and that his grace is sufficient for all our needs if we trust his action. We hear also that we were chosen by God in Christ before the foundation of the world, that Christ has become our shepherd, that he has made even us Gentiles members of his flock, and that he will sustain our lives.

When we realize that all of these announcements are only the beginning of the good news of Pentecost, it becomes very clear that we have been given joyful tidings to preach in this season of the church.

Our exegete for this volume is Dr. Leander E. Keck, dean and Winkley Professor of Biblical Theology at Yale Divinity School. A graduate of Andover Newton Theological School and Yale University, Dr. Keck has held New Testament posts at Vanderbilt and Emory Universities and is widely known as a lecturer, preacher, editor, and scholar. He is the author of numerous articles and books, two of the most recent being *The Bible in the Pulpit* and *Paul and His Letters*.

5

The Rev. Francis Wellford Hobbie, our homiletician, is the Benjamin Rice Lacy Professor of Pastoral Leadership and Homiletics at Union Theological Seminary in Virginia. Professor Hobbie has had wide experience in pastorates in Virginia, North Carolina, and Arkansas. He served as chairman of the General Assembly Mission Board of the Presbyterian Church in the United States and has taught Bible at Mary Baldwin College. He is the father of four children.

Richmond, Va.   ELIZABETH ACHTEMEIER

The Day of Pentecost

Lutheran	Roman Catholic	Episcopal	Pres/UCC/Chr	Meth/COCU
Ezek. 37:1–14	Acts 2:1–11	Acts 2:1–11 or Isa. 44:1–8	Joel 2:28–32	Acts 2:1–21 or Ezek. 37:1–14
Acts 2:1–21	1 Cor. 12:3b–7, 12–13	1 Cor. 12:4–13 or Acts 2:1–11	Acts 2:1–13	1 Cor. 12:4–13
John 7:37–39a	John 20:19–23	John 20:19–23 or John 14:8–17	John 16:5–15	John 16:5–15

EXEGESIS

Although the passages from Ezekiel, 1 Corinthians, and John all deal with the work of the divine Spirit, they are so diverse in scope and understanding that one should avoid trying to fuse them into a single "doctrine of the Holy Spirit." For Ezekiel, the point is that God's Spirit will vivify the "dead" people of God in exile. For Paul, the oneness of the Spirit is the basis of diversity in the church. John is concerned with the christological meaning of the experience of the Spirit.

First Lesson: Ezek. 37:1–14. The imagery of this passage is powerful and striking; one is reminded of the album covers for rock music. This imagery should be visualized and felt, not just analyzed and interpreted. Vv. 1–3 set the stage—a valley full of dry (bleached) bones. What could appear more dead? Vv. 4–6 report the absurd commission; vv. 7–10 tell how it was carried out in two steps, reminiscent of creation (Gen. 2:7). The oracle in vv. 11–14 interprets the foregoing vision. This remarkable vision (or was it a trance?) in vv. 1–10 is a promise that God will do the impossible—bring Israel out of exile. The prophet becomes the instrument through which God's word becomes effective: first sinews and flesh cover the dry bones, then life-breath (a pun: the same Hebrew word, *ruach,* means both wind and spirit) animates them. The return of the exiles (v. 12) is what the metaphor of opening the graves and imparting the Spirit to the corpses means. The promised return which Ezekiel had in view was almost certainly the return from Babylon;

interpreters debate whether the modern-day return is another fulfillment
of the promise. The vision rests on the assumption that the Spirit
animates, as the oracle actually says (v. 14). Ezekiel's own experience of
the Spirit is different—not animation but ecstatic vision. One should not
equate the metaphor of reanimation of the dead with the Christian
understanding of resurrection, which is transformation and not reanimation or resuscitation.

Second Lesson: 1 Cor. 12:4–13. This passage needs to be seen as
part of 1 Cor. 12—14, and these chapters, in turn, need to be seen in
relation to the trend in Corinth. Still debated is whether (and to what
extent) the Corinthians were involved in Gnostic (or proto-Gnostic)
tendencies or simply interpreted their experience of the Spirit in light of
long-established habits of dualistic thought which pitted the material
body against the immaterial (mental/spiritual) element in the self, or
were manifesting "enthusiasm"—an overly strong emphasis on the
presentness of salvation, which was believed to be attested to by the
experience of the Spirit, so that the "not yet" dimension of salvation
was eclipsed. It is unwise to force a choice between these three alternatives. That is, "enthusiasm" probably relied on dualistic concepts to
explain what was going on in glossolalia (tongue-speaking); the spiritual
element of the self made intense contact with the divine Spirit-power and
so escaped briefly the limitations of the body. Such a stance could also
lead to an outright Gnostic understanding. Paul has no interest in damp-
ening the vitality of this religious experience (1 Cor. 14:5, 18), but he
insists on interpreting it so that order will replace chaos (1 Cor. 14:26–
33), and unity and gratitude (1 Cor. 4:7) will replace divisive pride
(because some Spirit-released capacities are being prized more than
others).

In our passage Paul emphasizes the single source (the Spirit) of the
diverse gifts. The Spirit does not homogenize; he diversifies. Paul first
uses "body" as an analogy (v. 12)—Christ is *like* a body with diverse
organs (vv. 14–26); then he identifies the two—the church *is* the body of
Christ into which all have been baptized. Participation in the one body
through the Spirit ignores ethnic and social distinctions (v. 13).

Gospel: John 7:37–39. This is but a fragment of the Johannine
understanding of the Spirit, which is developed more fully in chaps.
13—17. Our pericope consists of a declaration (vv. 37–38) followed by
the narrator's interpretation. It is characteristic of John, but not of the
synoptics, that Jesus proclaimed himself as the bringer of salvation. The

feast (v. 37) is Tabernacles (Sukkot), which occurs in the fall (7:2). That the gift of the Spirit *follows* Jesus' glorification (= death) is emphasized in 16:7.

The exegetical problem in this passage centers in the declaration. Here it is clear that translations embody particular exegeses. The interpreter must decide whether the one from whom the "living water" flows is the believer (as in the RSV) or whether it is Jesus (as in JB). If the latter, then "who believes in me" is a parenthetical explanation of the thirsty person who comes to Jesus to drink (v. 37). If the former, then the person whose thirst is quenched by Jesus becomes the channel through which the "living water" flows to others. It is not clear which scripture is in view in v. 38, for no known OT text says what is here given as a quotation. For a good discussion of these problems in this passage and of the numerous possible interpretations, see Raymond E. Brown's commentary in the Anchor Bible series.

HOMILETICAL INTERPRETATION

First Lesson: Ezek. 37:1–14. Here the minister is before one of the most powerful images in the OT—Ezekiel's vision and oracle of the valley of dry bones, or the valley of death. Perhaps in a memory of a vast battlefield strewn everywhere with the bones of men long dead, or just in imagination, the prophet sees death filling his horizon, conveying to him the hopelessness, the despair of life cut off. But Ezekiel sees in the bleached bones the despair and hopelessness of a defunct nation. Israel is now crushed and in exile: all the great expectations and dreams of the nation destroyed, its once vaunted hope of national power and prestige ended, its capital city in ruins, its temple to its God a desolation. Before the prophet is the reality of the transient nature of human effort. The interpreter before this image needs to recapture vividly the impact of those who have lost all ground for hope if he or she is going to do justice to the affirmation, for it is against this backdrop of utter hopelessness that the affirmation is made.

The first insight is often overlooked: the prophet is no mere spectator of the transformation that follows—he is a participant. He must speak the word faithfully and not abandon his mission because there seems to be no hope for success. One would be insensitive indeed to fail to hear in this a unique word to all those.entrusted with mission.

Clearly, the main drive of the passage is not in the faithfulness of the prophet, but in the power of God to take a hopeless situation, a nation and a people defunct, and by his Spirit to bring new creation. "And I will put my Spirit within you, and you shall live. . . ." It is a message of hope for those who have lost all hope. It was for that day a message that the valley of dry bones, Israel, could be made alive again and return from exile through the power of God. As Karl Barth suggests (in *Church Dogmatics* III/1, p. 248), "One thing obviously was not killed and did not die when Israel became a valley of dry bones, and this was the prophetic Spirit by whom this people had become a nation—thus the same Spirit who had once quickened it and kept it alive was now to quicken it afresh after its necessary and merited disappearance. It was of this return of the breath of life to an Israel already dead that Ezekiel speaks."

The points of correlation between the passage and the church on Pentecost are quite obvious. A sermon could affirm that the church, as the people of God, receives life, indeed comes into being, not by human effort but by the act of God's Spirit. This is particularly significant in an age which seems to believe that the answer to the malaise of the churches is new structures or new organizations, as if the church were like any other ailing twentieth-century institution. All of this, of course, diverts attention from our basic need, the quickening power of God. Thus Pentecost affords us an opportunity to rediscover and reexamine the birth of the church and the potential rebirth of the church through the power of the Spirit.

But also a sermon on this passage may affirm a message of hope for all those who have lost all ground of hope. On the face of it, Israel in exile had no basis or expectation of hope, but the Spirit breathed on them, and they "stood on their feet an exceeding great army." There are times in the life of the church catholic or in the individual congregation when the ineffectiveness of the church, in the light of contemporary culture, fills us with despair. Does not the note need to be struck of the power of God to transform, renew, and re-create his people for their age? The history of the church affirms it; our passage undergirds it.

Second Lesson: 1 Cor. 12:4–13. This passage perhaps startles us as we prepare for the Day of Pentecost, for it is written in the context of a disturbing element—the possibility of a distortion of an understanding of the gifts of the Spirit creating divisiveness in the community. The early church recognized as gifts of the Spirit a wide diversity of abilities and functions (vv. 8–10). The difficulty in Corinth was with those who overemphasized certain gifts as giving them superiority over others. Paul saw and forcefully affirmed that the threat was not in diversity but in the struggle for superiority. Each within the community wished to set up his or her gift, his or her spiritual experience, as the epitome. "There arose a reasoning among them, which of them should be greatest" (Luke 22:24) is the basic threat to all communities; it is present whenever an attempt for community is made. Paul's response to the threat is to affirm the gifts in their diversity, but all from the same Spirit, and each con- tributing to the common good, to build up the community in love. The threat of divisiveness is met with a statement of the unifying power of the Spirit, leading to that great image of the unity of the body.

This passage could quite easily move in two directions for sermons. One would deal with the ancient, but not at all foreign, issue of the divisive potential of those who claim special gifts of the Spirit, strongly individualistic, contradicting the unity of the Spirit for the common good. This move would affirm all gifts but only as they witness to the one Spirit. The other would deal with the positive aspects of the Spirit witnessed here: its diverse gifts, its unifying power to overcome the deepest division between Jews and Greeks, slaves and free.

Gospel: John 7:37–39. Commentators have suggested a context for these words that makes them vivid: they are placed on the last day of the feast of Tabernacles, when there was a ceremony of drawing water accompanied by a reading from Isa. 12:3. In today's water-affluent society the force of the imagery may be lost, but in that ancient society with its scarcity of water the impact is understandable. It is in the context of that ceremony that Jesus, who has probably been sitting and teaching, stands and issues an invitation for those who thirst to come to him, the source of living water, for the gift of the Spirit. (The exegesis correctly calls attention to the lengthy and unresolved debate about who is the source; the preacher must "grasp the nettle" and make the decision on the best evidence.) Our affirmation is that Christ is the source and giver of the Spirit as part of his redemptive act, which is focused most clearly in the gift at Pentecost (Acts 2:1ff.).

The preacher may move with this passage too in several different directions. Most obviously, it affirms a gracious invitation to all who receive Christ's Spirit to find in him one who ministers to the barrenness of the human experience. The "living waters" imagery conveying its inexhaustible supply would be the main emphasis. Another possibility, quite dissimilar, is to emphasize the christological aspects of the Spirit in order to correct a modern-day distortion that elevates and separates the Spirit from his proper relation to the Christ. This approach would complement the material in 1 Cor. 12:4–13, correcting divisiveness of the Spirit.

The Holy Trinity
The First Sunday after Pentecost

Lutheran	Roman Catholic	Episcopal	Pres/UCC/Chr	Meth/COCU
Deut. 6:4–9	Deut. 4:32–34, 39–40	Exod. 3:1–6	Isa. 6:1–8	Deut. 4:32–34, 39–40
Rom. 8:14–17	Rom. 8:14–17	Rom. 8:12–17	Rom. 8:12–17	Rom. 8:12–17
John 3:1–17	Matt. 28:16–20	John 3:1–16	John 3:1–8	John 3:1–17

EXEGESIS

First Lesson: Deut. 6:4–9. This is surely one of the most important paragraphs in the OT. V. 4 became *the* theological affirmation of Judaism; known as the Shema (from the first word, "Hear!"), it was recited twice daily by the devout. Jesus combined v. 5 with Lev. 19:18 to form the answer to the question concerning the great commandment (Mark 12:29–31). Vv. 8–9 came to be taken literally, and so provided the scriptural warrant for religious customs: (*a*) the phylacteries (small cube-shaped receptacles for Scriptures) are tied on the wrist and forehead; (*b*) the mezuzah (a small tube-like receptacle for a tiny scroll) is fastened to the doorpost. On the Holy Trinity it is appropriate that Christians identify themselves with that text which became the epitome of unyielding monotheism; however difficult the doctrine of the Trinity may be, Christians have not understood it as a compromise of monotheism—as if God were understood to be a committee.

The footnotes to modern versions like the RSV show that v. 4 can be translated in more than one way. More important, the juxtaposition of v. 5 and v. 4 suggests that the oneness of God should elicit undivided love. The whole self is to love the one God—a theme emphasized in Deuteronomy (for example, 10:12; 11:13; 13:3). Tacitly, the text affirms that the individual's love for God is nourished in community: v. 4 is addressed to the people; v. 7 emphasizes the transmission of value and tradition to the next generation. Love for God is to be nurtured by a conscious and continuous chain of remembrance of God's law and of God's initiative in the Exodus (Deut. 6:20–25 explicates v. 7; see also Exod. 13:8–10). Thereby Deuteronomy shows that it is not interested in mere compliance but rather in true obedience centered in the will (heart) and understanding, grounded in gratitude, and manifested in a sensitized conscience for the neighbor (Deut. 5:6–7; 10:12—11:1; 27:9–10). If Deut. 6:4–9 is observed, Deut. 30:11–14 will be true. All the commandments are, for Deuteronomy as for Jesus, really elaborations of what love for God entails.

Second Lesson: Rom. 8:12–17. This remarkable, compact paragraph combines a tacit exhortation (vv. 12–13), a general declaration (v. 14), and an explanation which opens out onto the future (vv. 15–17). The concern in v. 12 links the paragraph with 8:1–11, and the concluding reference to suffering links it with the verses that follow. Consequently, sermons which emerge from the beginning or end of the passage should consider the appropriate adjacent passage as well. Note that Paul himself interprets the general declaration (which might be a traditional formulation) about the "sons of God" in nonmale terms (vv. 14, 16–17).

The tension between "flesh" and "Spirit" must be understood as Paul understood it. Unfortunately, the NEB translates "flesh" as "lower nature" (our physicality)—which is precisely what Paul did *not* mean. For Paul, "flesh" is that which is creaturely, finite, phenomenal, physical when it has become perverted into a field of force, a domain of power, a system of values and constraints (for example, as when sexual drives are distorted into lust). "Flesh" is creaturehood gone wrong. "Spirit," in turn, is not one's "higher nature" (human spirit) but the divine field of force. The struggle between "flesh" and "Spirit" is not between higher and lower natures, between incommensurate components of the self, but between two spheres of power which compete for the allegiance of the self. When Paul writes of putting to death the deeds of the body, he does not mean throttling bodily drives as such; rather he refers to the concrete deeds done by one's physical self under the dominance of fleshly power. One lives according to flesh or Spirit.

Paul's main concern is to indicate what life according to the Spirit entails. It is a matter of being led by the divine Presence, and it is also the boldness to call God *Abba* (the Aramaic word which Paul translates as "Father" means "Papa"; see also Gal. 4:6). It is not clear that Paul is here thinking of the Lord's Prayer. More important, Paul interprets what it means to address God intimately, as a child would address a parent— this is the work of the Spirit, not an inference from creation. Thus the Spirit is the inner Presence which attests that the relation to God has been made right, rectified (which is what justification means). Those whose relation to God is rectified are now related to God as child to parent, not as slave to alien master (flesh). The last phrase in v. 17 is difficult, for it appears to attach a condition to being co-heirs with Christ

(RSV: "provided that . . ."); it is more likely that the meaning is "if indeed," or "since" (the same word is used in v. 9).

Gospel: John 3:1–17. This complex pericope twice illustrates John's device of using a word with a double meaning: first, a wrong meaning whereby a person misunderstands Jesus; second, a simple pun. The first double meaning turns on *anōthen* ("over again," or "from above"). Jesus speaks of being born "from above," through the Spirit, but Nicodemus takes it as "over again"—from the womb (vv. 3–4). The second double meaning turns on *pneuma,* which means both "wind" and "Spirit" (v. 8), and on "lift up" (v. 14).

V. 6 sets flesh and Spirit over against each other, but not as Paul did in Romans 8. Paul wanted to bring out the struggle of Christian experience, to emphasize living *according* to flesh or Spirit; John wants to contrast flesh and Spirit as alternate grounds of one's being. From what is your existence really derived?—That is John's question. For John, flesh is not creaturehood gone wrong but creaturehood as such—the finite, the phenomenal (thus "the Word became flesh"). The one whose life is derived from the Spirit lives by that. There is no path from the former to the latter; there is only the shift from the one to the other, so drastic that it can be spoken of as birth. Paul too sees that "flesh and blood cannot inherit the kingdom" (1 Cor. 15:50), but Paul sees the solution in the transformation of one's total being at the Parousia, when the dead shall be raised and the living "changed." For John, there is no need to wait—the solution is a new beginning now in which one is born "from above"—by the Spirit. John 5:25–29 shows that the Fourth Gospel also contains a futurist eschatology, but the real emphasis is on the possibility of new life now. John 5:24 shows that this new life ("eternal life") is available now. Although it includes life after death and assumes that this life is endless, the real point about "eternal" life lies elsewhere—it is qualitatively different.

Vv. 13–15 introduce another theme. The logic is indirect. (*a*) The Son of man descended from heaven (to earth) and then returned (ascended). This is a characteristically Johannine way of understanding who Jesus really is. (*b*) The "lifting up" of the Son of man begins with the crucifixion, which marks the beginning of the Son's return (ascent) to the Father (17:11). (*c*) This lifting up on a pole is like the lifting up of the serpent on a pole in Moses' day (Num. 21:9). Just as the Israelites who looked to the serpent were saved, so those who look to the Son of man on the cross will be saved: they will have eternal life. Thus Nicodemus's question in v. 9 is answered: eternal life is possible because of Jesus' death which begins his return to God. Vv. 16–17 begin a comment on the Christ-event.

HOMILETICAL INTERPRETATION

First Lesson: Deut. 6:4–9. At first glance it seems strange, but then transparently clear, why on Trinity Sunday, the day set aside for consideration of this basic Christian doctrine, we are considering this passage. This passage emphasizes Israel's unyielding stand for one God against all attempts to accept a pantheon of gods. Israel's devotion is undivided: twice daily and in the opening of every synagogue service, the Shema is said as a rallying point of monotheism. The appropriateness of it here is to stand against any distortion of the Christian doctrine which divides God into three Gods or emphasizes one aspect of the Trinity at the expense of the unity. This is not just some ancient debate. A few years ago, when the Presbyterian Church in the United States was writing a modern declaration of the faith, members of the committee were asked to define a modern major distortion of the faith confronting the church in this age. One area of general agreement was the tendency of the church to move toward an emphasis upon Jesus—a kind of "Jesus-olatry," disregarding God as Creator or as Sustainer. The danger is ever before the church to fragment the oneness of God, to elevate the Holy Spirit's work above the work of the Father and Son, or to set the Son's love against the Father's justice. The Christian minister on this day, with the powerful words of the Shema echoing, could well affirm the unity of God's being and work—resisting the separation of the work of God as Creator from the work of God as Redeemer. It is certainly not strange at all on Trinity Sunday for the Christian pulpit to affirm unyielding commitment to the opening words of the Shema.

Another insight provided by the passage and highlighted by the exegesis may capture the attention of the preacher. That is, the proper response to the act of God's redeeming love at Sinai is a response, in love, of the total person to God. The concept, of course, is totally familiar to the minister, being the first part of Jesus' summary of the Law. But here there are several emphases often overlooked. The first is the way this response to God's initial love is freed of sentimental emotionalism by being united to keeping "these words which I command you this day," in essence, the Decalogue. In a sense we become like the persons we love, taking from them characteristics and styles of life. So, in a quite profound manner, we become like the one we worship. Our love for God is reflected in being like him, mirroring in our lives his

ways. In a culture where most guideposts have been obliterated—
where, as the angel Gabriel reports to God in *Green Pastures,* "everything not nailed down is coming loose"—a recovery of commandments
and precepts to give directions and purpose to life may be a note of
grace.

A second emphasis, one often overlooked, is that this love of God is
sustained and nurtured in community. While the individual alone makes
the decision of faith, faith cannot be sustained by the individual in
isolation. Love for God is sustained in the community of faith that tells
and retells its stories of who it is and what it is to be.

The preacher dealing with this passage has a variety of choices: to
speak of our monotheism as opposed to the distortions of the Trinity; to
speak of our response in love to God's love; or to speak of the importance of community in nurturing the love of God.

Second Lesson: Rom. 8:12–17. The selection of this passage for
Trinity Sunday is also obvious, containing as it does suggestions of the
Trinitarian formula. The minister, however, would be well advised to
follow the lead of the passage and not try to explain the who and the why
of the Father, Son, and Holy Spirit but to concentrate on what they do.
The pulpit needs to recapture the exciting language of the NT which
deals not with formulas of the Trinity but with the impact of its truth in
creating new life, new relationships.

Here in this passage, Paul speaks of that moment in the work of the
Spirit when life's center shifts, so that the allegiance of self is to the
spiritual way of life and no longer to its fatal opposite. This movement is
described in the imagery of being freed from fear and slavery under one
master and being set into a new relation with another, a God who is a
loving Father. This new relationship, which God creates by his Spirit,
enables us to utter the simple but intimate and far-reaching exclamation,
"Abba! Father!" The word "abba" expresses the deepest trust and
affection of a child for a loved parent and here mirrors the new relationships that we have as children of God and as his heirs. This term "heirs
of God" should not be understood as an artificial and cold legal formulation contradicting the intimacy of the "Abba! Father!" exclamation.
Rather, the preacher needs to grasp the meaning of the word to the
Roman readers. For them an adopted child is a chosen child. Paul is
thinking about God's deliberate choice, out of love, of a person to be his
child. But also, an adopted child, to the Romans, is not an inferior child.
For example, a Roman emperor would sometimes adopt a child to be his
successor, seeing in the selected "son" one more deserving to be

emperor than a natural son. Thus the term, rather than diminishing, heightens the sense of radical transformation taking place in the person who senses God as the loving Father accepting us as his children. This occurs, not as a result of reasoned discovery, but as a gift of God's grace through the Spirit.

The minister is immediately aware of the points of correlation between the passage and the congregation. We are also a people in slavery, mastered by concepts of life that produce not sought-for fulfillment but fear and death. Indeed, the phrase most often used to describe our time is "the age of anxiety." We are living lives faced in the wrong direction. The passage speaks to this basic need and affirms that nothing less will do than a change in the orientation of life. This occurs when we realize, through the Spirit, that we may know ourselves as loved by God and that our lives have purpose in the Creation. We realize then that the power behind the universe wills good for us and that nothing can take us from him.

Gospel: John 3:1–17. Nothing can grasp the attention of the people more effectively than a well-told story. This story of Jesus and Nicodemus has a drama and poignancy which the preacher should consider utilizing. Nicodemus, the ruler of the Pharisees, in coming to Jesus "by night" suggests a seeking spirit with unanswered questions who desires some insight from Jesus but is uneasy lest he be observed. The conversation between the two illustrates how people can fail to communicate because they are talking on two different levels of understanding. Jesus' statement "except a man be born again" speaks of the necessity of being born "from above" through the Spirit. But Nicodemus, literal-minded and in a sense earthbound in his concepts, misunderstands and goes off on the tangent of the impossibility of a literal second birth in the flesh. Jesus leads him back to the more profound meaning, the necessity for a person to be born of the Spirit. Nicodemus's final response in the narrative remains at the earthbound level: "How can these things be?" This response also seems to mirror the modern mind, anchored to what can be seen and observed, devoid of a comprehension of the realm of the Spirit. Jesus at this point mildly rebukes him by observing that as a ruler of Israel Nicodemus does not know these things, and tells him in vv. 14–17 the heart of the Gospel.

Anyone should be hesitant to presume to suggest how a preacher should deal with this passage. So rich is it in possibilities that it would be presumptuous to choose one way to deal with it; v. 16 itself has probably been one of the most-preached verses in the Bible. However, the juxtaposition of this passage with the passage from Romans, when preached in the context of Trinity Sunday, would suggest, on this occasion, that the central affirmation be the power of the Spirit to create newness—rebirth from above—regardless of the status or age of the person. So here the attention might be centered upon the drastic transforming power of the Spirit to begin anew with human life. Again, the way to this newness is not through human effort; not even a ruler of the Pharisees, skilled in interpreting the law, can find or even grasp the meaning of it. When newness of life comes, it is a breaking into human life beyond any intellectual quest. This is a word indeed for moderns, who imagine all things within their grasp and yet who have lost the sense of the breaking in of a power "from above."

The Second Sunday after Pentecost

Lutheran	Roman Catholic	Episcopal	Pres/UCC/Chr	Meth/COCU
Deut. 5:12–15	Deut. 5:12–15	Deut. 5:6–21	Deut. 5:12–15	Deut. 5:12–15
2 Cor. 4:5–12	2 Cor. 4:6–11	2 Cor. 4:5–12	2 Cor. 4:6–11	2 Cor. 4:5–12
Mark 2:23–28	Mark 2:23—3:6 or Mark 2:23–28	Mark 2:23–28	Mark 2:23—3:6	Mark 2:23—3:6

EXEGESIS

First Lesson: Deut. 5:12–15. This is but one of a number of passages which command Sabbath observance, each of which represents a somewhat different understanding of why work should cease on the last day of the week. In fact, Exod. 34:21 gives no explanation at all, though it does insist that Sabbath is to be observed even during the busiest time of the year for farmers! Embedded in another collection of laws in Exod. 23:10–19 is a Sabbath law (v. 12) like that of our pericope; it too emphasizes that Sabbath is to be observed for the well-being of work animals, servants, and resident aliens. In the Holiness Code (Leviticus 17—26) Israel is commanded to "keep my Sabbath" (Lev. 19:3); it is God's day, and observing it free of work (assumed here) is one of the ways by which Israel becomes a holy people (19:1). According to the Priestly creation story, the seventh day was made holy by God, who inaugurated Sabbath observance. This is also the belief expressed in the Decalogue in Exod. 20:8–11. Deut. 5:12–15 on the other hand offers a quite different reason for ceasing work on the last day of the week: because Israel had been in servitude in Egypt, the Sabbath should be the weekly reminder of emancipation. Remembering the Exodus is a major theme in Deuteronomy (for example, 6:20–25; 8:11–20).

Three things are to be noted in light of this overview. First, none of this legislation connects Sabbath observance with religious activity at a shrine or temple (as in Num. 28:9–10), nor do the Psalms mention the Sabbath (except the superscription to Psalm 92). Not until the rise of the synagogue did the Sabbath become the date of a weekly assembly of the congregation. Second, Exod. 20:8–11 and Deut. 5:12–15 spell out in detail who is to rest, evidently to make clear that one cannot require others to work while claiming to be observant oneself. Third, all Sabbath legislation takes for granted a society whose economy *can* come to a standstill on the same day each week.

Second Lesson: 2 Cor. 4:5–12. This pericope, which concerns Paul's self-interpretation as a bearer of the gospel centered in Christ's cross/resurrection, is part of an extended discussion with the Corinthian church. From 3:7 on, Paul's language alludes to the story of Moses' appearance on Mount Sinai in Exod. 34:33ff. So in v. 6 of our lesson, the "glory of God in the face of Christ" adopts the imagery of that same story.

The main part of the lesson (vv. 7–11) concerns the disparity between what is manifest in Paul (weakness and suffering) and what is also present, though hidden like a jewel in a clay pot. In what was once part of an earlier letter, Paul dealt with the same theme and did so with a note of irony (2 Cor. 11:21—12:10). In this passage, however, he is not ironic but contrasts his experience with his inner attitude toward it. He understands his vulnerability as embodying what Jesus' death means for him—no special favors, no immunity from suffering. The "life of Jesus" which is thereby manifest in Paul's mortal body is the transcendent resurrection life—the "nevertheless" of persistent hope which exists in the midst of suffering. Paul does not "come on strong," always smiling and always succeeding. Were that the case, he would indeed preach himself as Exhibit A (v. 5), pointing to his own success as a sure sign of salvation. Actually, becoming a Christian did not make life enchanted for Paul; it made his life harder. Nonetheless, through such a figure, the gospel of Jesus' cross/resurrection was brought to others. So it is clear that the gospel was not about Paul's endurance, ability to "keep his cool," or success; rather it was the hidden grace of God working through him. Thus it was that Paul appropriated cross/resurrection to interpret his life's work—not as "cross now, crown later" but as the hiddenness of transcendent power and grace in the midst of weakness and pain.

In v. 12 the contrast between death and life (= cross/resurrection) is no longer applied to Paul's own actual existence (his body) but is "apportioned" between Paul and the readers: death in Paul, life in them. The suffering he endures is to enhance the role of the resurrection life among the readers. As v. 15 says, "it is all for your sake."

Gospel: Mark 2:23–28. (Matt. 12:1–8 and Luke 6:1–5 tell the story somewhat differently.) It is widely believed that Mark incorporated a collection of conflict stories (2:1—3:6), one of which is our story. But before that cycle of stories was collected, when our story was circulating orally, it had come to include three answers to the question put to Jesus in v. 24. Each answer is complete in itself and does not require the others. Putting them side by side intensifies the point that the followers of Jesus are right in adopting a freer attitude toward the Sabbath.

The first answer (vv. 25–26) is an appeal to precedent (1 Sam. 21:1–6): David himself violated the rules in the face of human need (we do not know why Mark has the wrong priest). Hence, Jesus' disciples can be excused because they were hungry (a point not made explicit in Mark but supplied by Matthew). The introductory formula "and he said to them" (v. 27) shows that the second answer was once independent of its present setting, for it would be unnecessary if Jesus had kept on speaking. This answer is standard teaching of the Pharisees themselves; therefore, they ought to acknowledge it. The third answer (v. 28) is ambiguous in the mouth of Jesus but clear in the early Christians' minds. For them, the Son of man is Jesus. His exalted status gives him the right to be "Lord" even of the Sabbath—to legitimate the freer Christian observance. On the lips of Jesus, however, Son of man is ambiguous: it can mean either "human being" or the "Son of man" (the heavenly Judge and Regent). If the former, then v. 28 is virtually a paraphrase of v. 27. If the latter, then Jesus tacitly claims to be the Son of man and so asserts his right to legitimate Christian Sabbath observances. One should reflect on what each answer does and does not imply about Christian attitudes toward Sunday.

HOMILETICAL INTERPRETATION

First Lesson: Deut. 5:12–15. This lesson deals with the observance of the Sabbath, giving the basis of the observance of the day and the responses made by the believer. The Sabbath is based upon what God has done for Israel in the Exodus-event. On this day Israel is to remember when it was a people who were no people, a slave people, who then by God's act of redemption were rescued from slavery. The preacher should reflect upon the significant role remembrance plays in biblical faith. This gift of remembrance—to think back, to re-create in imagination an historical event—provides both a focus and a motivation for faith for Jew and Christian. Throughout Israel's history, the Exodus is the historical event signaling God's gracious act and motivating Israel to respond in gratitude.

Israel's remembrance issues out in grateful response, from the vantage point of the passage, in two ways. First, there is the response of setting the day apart for rest. Humankind is the beneficiary, for the commandment recognizes the basic human need for rest from labor. It speaks a significant word for our culture caught up in obsessive work, turning even our so-called leisure time into busy activities, seeking oblivion. The exegete has noted that the passage does not point to religious observances, rituals to be kept to mark this day. The preacher would do well to refrain from using the passage as an occasion to lay upon the listeners the demand for church attendance but should emphasize the "grace note" of this day of remembrance.

Second, there is a response of humanitarian concern for others: one's children, one's servants, strangers, even one's cattle and beasts of burden are to be afforded rest. Thus we are reminded that Israel's affirmations of faith are inseparable from its ethical sensitivity. Israel's faith moves naturally in the horizontal plane of relationships: its grateful response to God is seen in relation to neighbor and to the creation.

This passage may move in many directions. On the eve of vacation time it may be used to emphasize a rediscovery of rest, as God's gracious gift, or it may be used to affirm the central place of remembrance in faith: for Israel, in redemption from captivity, and for Christians, in redemption at the cross. But the primary significance of the passage for the preacher may be as backdrop and resource to the Marcan passage for the day.

Second Lesson: 2 Cor. 4:5–12. This lesson, a part of a larger passage extending back to previous chapters, is an assertion of Paul's credentials as an apostle made against those questioning his authority. Paradoxically, his claim is based not upon his gifts or upon any personal strength but upon a catalog of his sufferings (vv. 8–9). Paul shows that the treasure of the gospel is entrusted to a weak vessel so that one might know that it is not the power of human personality or the attractiveness and persuasiveness of the messenger that is the power, but that the power comes from the gospel message of Jesus Christ—this is the power of God (cf. 1. Cor. 2:1–5). What a paradox this must have been in the early church! Paul's adversaries base their credentials upon visions and ecstasies; Paul, upon a life of suffering. What a greater paradox it is to us in this day when the Christian faith is presented by many of its messengers as the guarantee of the fulfilled life, the successful life. Religious TV is filled with hucksters for the faith testifying to what Christianity has done for them and presenting their "successes" as evidences for the Christian faith. Imagine, in contrast, an interview with Paul saying, "We are afflicted, perplexed, crushed." It is not likely he would be popular on religious talk shows, but that is his point: "What we preach is not ourselves but Jesus Christ as Lord."

There is another, a positive, dimension of this life of suffering to be marked. It is that suffering in obedience to the faith mirrors Jesus' life. Jesus' life clearly was not characterized by the usual indexes of success and happiness, but rather it was a "cross-shaped" life. Paul affirms the role of the believer whose life, marked by suffering, points to and reminds one of his suffering Lord. Thus, not only does the passage present the paradox of the suffering life being the life bearing unique credentials, but it also declares that such a life contains within itself a powerful pointer to the crucified Lord.

A sermon could demonstrate the relevance of the passage to the contemporary listener by contrasting the shallowness of modern "success stories" of the Christian faith with Paul's witness of the marks of his suffering apostleship. The passage also may speak to a church's discouragement at not being "successful," pointing out that the power rests in the message and not in the earthen vessel. In addition, the passage is a profile of the purpose of the minister. A minister who served innumerable churches over forty years would always, on the first Sunday in the pulpit of the new church, proclaim v. 5 as the purpose for ministry: "to preach Jesus Christ as Lord and himself as their servant for Jesus' sake."

Gospel: Mark 2:23–28. To heighten understanding, the preacher would be well advised to place this passage in juxtaposition with the Deuteronomy passage. There the Sabbath is seen as a response to God's gracious act and is oriented to human need. In this vignette from Mark, Sabbath observance has been distorted and loaded down with innumerable restrictions, making it burdensome and restrictive to humanity. This is vividly presented by the Pharisees' objection to the plucking of the heads of wheat, when even the law itself in Deut. 23:25 makes such acts permissible. The Pharisees, strict legalists as they were, however, saw this activity as a part of harvesting, which was forbidden. In the story they represent what happens when form or ritual is divorced from meaning. The Pharisees insist upon strict observances, but the reason for observance has largely been lost. No longer is the Sabbath a gift; it is a burden. Jesus' presence and his words are the rediscovery of the original meaning of the Sabbath. He is Lord of the Sabbath, rediscovering it for humanity. As Lord of the Sabbath, he removes the burden of the Sabbath for humanity and gives the Sabbath back as a gracious gift. As Lord of the Sabbath, Jesus frees humanity to see laws and regulations in their proper perspective, as aids for life; designed for humanity, they are to be set aside in times of critical human need.

The preacher must guard against the danger of interpreting this in a humanistic way so that Sabbath law or any religious observance is to be kept or broken as it best serves humanitarian interests. The focal point is Christ: it is not what is well-pleasing to us and serves our purposes, but what is pleasing to Christ and serves his purposes.

But what does the twentieth-century preacher do with this passage? He or she knows that no longer do we celebrate Jewish Sabbath, centered upon the remembrance of the Exodus-event, but that our Sunday marks the coming of the salvation-event in Christ. Clearly, the minister also knows that the situation regarding Sunday in most denominations is not a legal "Sabbatarianism" but a nonobservance of the day. We are freed from legalism as regards Sunday, but, unfortunately, we have been "freed" also from the graciousness of the gift and its meaning for humanity. The preacher may do well to rediscover the day as a day of remembrance and celebration of God's gracious act of salvation issuing out in humanitarian concern. The meaning of worship may be investigated, as it has become ritual and lost its center.

The Third Sunday after Pentecost

Lutheran	Roman Catholic	Episcopal	Pres/UCC/Chr	Meth/COCU
Gen. 3:9–15	Gen. 3:9–15	Gen. 3:(1–7) 8–21	Gen. 3:9–15	Gen. 3:1–21
2 Cor. 4:13–18	2 Cor. 4:13—5:1	2 Cor. 4:13–18	2 Cor. 4:13—5:1	2 Cor. 4:13—5:1
Mark 3:20–35	Mark 3:20–35	Mark 3:20–35	Mark 3:20–35	Mark 3:20–35

EXEGESIS

First Lesson: Gen. 3:1–21. This story became more important in postbiblical Judaism and in Christianity than it was in the OT or in Hebrew faith. True, the story stands near the beginning of the Book of Beginnings; still, the rest of the OT makes virtually no reference to this story, and the reasons given for Israel's or humanity's sin do not place blame on Adam or Eve or the serpent. There is no equivalent in the OT to 4 Ezra (2 Esdras) 7:48: "O Adam, what have you done? For though it was you who sinned, the fall was not yours alone, but ours also who are your descendants." Note that "fall" is a word that appears neither in our story nor in Paul's use of it (Rom. 5:12–21); it is a way of regarding what happened. The significance of this story is enhanced when we remember that several other options have come down to us. One option blames the human plight on "fallen angels" (developing the obscure story in Gen. 6:1–4). Another traces the human condition to the creator, who was a deity inferior to the God of Jesus Christ. The "genius" of Genesis 3, which finally became the dominant view, is that it locates responsibility on the human pair and does not blame either Satan or an incompetent creator.

Against the background of chap. 2, the story moves in clearly defined stages: vv. 1–7 report the disobedience and its immediate consequence; vv. 8–19 tell of God's response, first in confronting the couple, then in the threefold punishment (serpent, woman, Adam); v. 20 explains the woman's name by anticipating chap. 4; and v. 21 reports God's mercy before the expulsion recounted in vv. 22–24—God replaced the scant covering of fig leaves with garments of skins. Vv. 14–19 probably had an independent origin; they are etiological in character—that is, they explain why the serpent is hated (overlooking the fact that the serpent was sometimes revered) and why it slithers on the ground; why women, in apparent contrast with animals, experience pain in childbirth yet desire sex with men; why society became male-dominated; and why, in contrast with animals, only humans must toil to survive. The kind of society which the storyteller took for granted is clear.

It is not clear why the serpent approached the woman instead of Adam. Perhaps it was because she was vulnerable to doubt, for she learned of God's command only through Adam (she had not yet been created when God identified the prohibited tree). The woman was not motivated by a desire to gain advantage over Adam; she shared the fruit. The immediate results were a loss of innocence (awareness of nakedness) and a makeshift countermeasure. The story implies that knowledge of good and evil and loss of innocence go together. Goodness and obedience are no longer spontaneous and natural but now are the result of choice and struggle against the alternative. Morality is possible only on this side of the Fall.

Second Lesson: 2 Cor. 4:13–18. This lesson partly continues, in vv. 13–15, the discussion of last Sunday's Second Lesson and partly introduces a new subject which is treated more fully in next Sunday's Second Lesson.

Grammatically, vv. 13–14 consist of two clauses which give reasons why, and the conditions under which, Paul speaks the gospel. The first claims that Ps. 116:10 (in Septuagint, 115:10) is true also of Paul—he speaks because he believes; he speaks out of faith, not out of an innate capacity to endure suffering (see 4:7–12). The second refers to the hope of the resurrection, which will unite Jesus, Paul, and the readers in the presence of God the Resurrector. The former clause links Paul's work with the past (Scripture), the latter with the definitive future. Together they constitute the horizons of Paul's sense of accountability. V. 15 rounds this out.

Rhetorical contrasts dominate vv. 16–18: outer self/inner self, affliction/glory, things seen/things not seen, temporary/eternal. The contrast between the inner and the outer self is suggestive, not precise. Although Paul's language is close to a body-spirit duality, he probably means that outwardly the whole self is passing away while inwardly the whole self is being renewed. (Literally, Paul writes of the "outer man," [*anthropos*, not *anēr* = "male"] and the "inner man.") It seems as if Paul is deliberately avoiding the language of a body-spirit dualism, while recognizing that there is indeed a nonphenomenal self which is being renewed by the Spirit.

Paul's point in v. 17 is developed more fully, and somewhat differently, in Rom. 8:18–25. The idea (in v. 18) that what is visible is transient (and hence not very important in the long run) whereas what is invisible is eternal (and hence truly important) is not original with Paul. From this he concludes that the brief, present experience of suffering is hardly comparable with the eternal, future glory. At the same time, he continues with another common theme, the pedagogical use of suffering— suffering prepares, trains, makes one fit for the glorious future.

Gospel: Mark 3:20–35. This passage brings together various traditions about Jesus' mental state. In Mark these traditions introduce the theme of the division—for or against—which Jesus precipitates. In the pre-Marcan development of the material, vv. 28–30 were added because they were appropriate to the general subject matter. As the text now stands, there are three charges leveled against Jesus. The first charge was that "his folks" regarded him as "beside himself" (v. 21), to which the story returns in vv. 31–35. Whether Mark used two separate incidents (v. 21 and vv. 31–35) to compose the whole passage, or whether he inferred v. 21 from vv. 31–35, is not clear. In v. 22 the scribes make the second and third accusations: Beelzebub has Jesus in his control, and Jesus uses Beelzebub (the chief demon) to cast out demons.

The charges are answered in reverse order. To the third charge, Jesus replies (v. 23) with a terse counterquestion: "How can Satan exorcise Satan?" The accusation self-destructs. Vv. 24–26 elaborate the point. To the second charge, Jesus replies by turning the accusation around: Jesus can invade the demons' stronghold only because the master of the realm has been bound (v. 27). Thus this charge too self-destructs. Jesus implicitly claims that his exorcisms show he has bound Beelzebub. (Some regard Mark 1:12–13 as a hint of this.) That vv. 28–30 were attached to v. 27 is clear from the opening formula, especially because v. 30 gives the reason. Unfortunately, Mark does not explain why blaspheming against the Spirit is so much more serious than blaspheming against Jesus. One should be cautious in trying to fill the gap. To the first charge, Jesus replies by reconstituting the community which has a claim on him (vv. 31–35).

HOMILETICAL INTERPRETATION

First Lesson: Gen. 3:1–21. The story of the loss of paradise is one of a number of stories found in the first chapters of Genesis explaining how things came to be as they are and providing a backdrop of the human situation against which the drama of human salvation will be played, beginning in Genesis 12:1. About these events (described here in legend form) someone has written, "These things never were, but always are." They hold up before us a distant mirror in which we see ourselves more clearly than we perhaps would desire.

Here is described the theological reason why the intended harmonious relation between God and humanity is distorted and fragmented, the reasons for the chaos of troubled life which surrounds us today, on both the individual and the universal scale. The origin of this tragedy in the story comes not from outside the creation in some devil figure; it mysteriously originates in the world through humanity: man and woman share equally in the breaking of the harmony. The event is told in the simple kindergarten language of a tree and forbidden fruit and a talking snake, but it conveys the essence of our dilemma. Adam, though in paradise, is restless with any limitation set upon his life, and he rebels against his status as creature, repudiates trust and obedience to the Creator, and takes from the forbidden tree. The story shows us as we are. Our nature rejects the docile role, desiring to be not merely creature, but creator. Milton understood the drive of the human heart: "Better to reign in hell than serve in heaven" (*Paradise Lost*). But Adam's reaching for the forbidden tree to exert his will over that of the Creator ends in misery; every aspect of life, once intended as blessing, now becomes distorted and irretrievably lost. Redemption lies outside the story; our chaotic life, however, is God's reminder that we have lost our way.

The preacher has no difficulty in demonstrating the relevance of this story. It is as relevant as—no, much more relevant than—the morning newspaper at our breakfast tables. The challenge before the preacher is to prevent the structure of the legend from obscuring the truths "that always are"; far too many are diverted by talking snakes and fig leaves from the insights into the human dilemma that the story presents. This passage speaks to a humanity that assumes no limitations upon its creatureliness, that believes it can transcend finiteness and "become as God." It is this will to power, forgetting Creator and obedience and trust, that disturbs the harmony of creation. The preacher walks a razor's edge here lest he or she be heard speaking against the quest of the human mind and spirit. Certainly the grandeur of our humanity is in our probing search for new insights, but our despair is in our loss of the One who gives stability and meaning to our existence.

Second Lesson: 2 Cor. 4:13–18. The passage cannot be isolated; it must be placed in the larger context of Paul's thought, which goes back to last Sunday's lesson. This passage centers upon a word of hope, despite the fact that the external evidence points toward defeat and despair. Clearly, there is external evidence in the catalog of Paul's ministry in vv. 8–9 that would lead one to lose heart. Beyond that, there is the poignant note that Paul recognizes the reality of a wasting away of life. He has faced the threat of sudden death in his ministry, but now he faces the inevitable diminishing of strength, reminding him of his mortality. In the face of all this, Paul affirms his hope—a hope not based upon his own strength or abilities, but a hope that the One whose power raised the Lord Jesus from the dead will also raise him with Jesus. This hope is not centered only upon some future act on God's part, but it is a hope in the resurrection power that can renew daily the resources of life, even when life is slipping away. Paul comprehends this because he sees reality beyond the visible, material evidences of life, refusing to be limited only to what can be seen or heard or measured.

Few ministers close to a congregation fail to sense the presence of despair in the lives of people. This despair takes many forms but clearly is like the despair in this passage. There is a despair that the objective evidences of life indicate the defeat of all that is true and good. There is despair in the evidences of the weakening of our physical bodies, of approaching death, seeming to prove that life is not worth living and that our best efforts and deep affections go for nothing. In addition to this, the preacher is aware that he or she lives in the midst of a culture where reality and truth are based only upon what can be seen and measured. The challenge, in this context, is to speak a word that precisely here is the great dividing line between religion and no religion. Faith sees beyond the present reality of defeat and death, sees things that are unseen. Faith affirms Christ's resurrection from the dead and sees in his resurrection the promise of ours, "so we do not lose heart."

Gospel: Mark 3:20–35. The minister before this passage may seek for some unifying theme or idea amid the heterogeneity of its parts. A clue may be found by placing it in a broader context.

Prior to this passage, Mark recounts certain events underscoring the power of Jesus. In this passage Mark introduces a growing opposition. This opposition takes many different forms; in this lesson it centers upon the accusation that Jesus has lost his mind. His friends or relatives are concerned about his well-being (vv. 20–21, 31), and the scribes use the accusations maliciously (v. 22). Both groups seem to be unaware of something new breaking into the world—a new relationship, a new "family" based upon those responding to Jesus and doing the will of God (vv. 31–35).

At the center of this opposition to Jesus is the accusation of the ecclesiastical authorities that Jesus is in league with the forces of evil. The strange charge (with its distorted logic, so clearly demolished by Jesus) provides an insight into Jesus' struggle with evil. Here Jesus affirms that he is involved in a struggle against evil, overthrowing evil powers that enslave people. The struggle is real, though the issue is not in doubt; the forces of evil will be overcome and ultimately bound.

Introduced in the struggle with the scribes is Jesus' comment on the "unpardonable sin." This concept creates misunderstanding and is the source of such mental anguish among sensitive people in precarious mental health that it must be treated with extreme caution. Two basic points should be made: (1) the saying is preceded in v. 30 with the statement of the unbelievable breadth of God's grace, and (2) the saying is found in the context of those who deliberately stand in opposition, wishing to destroy Jesus. Those concerned for fear they have committed this sin do not fall under its judgment.

The passage closes (vv. 31–35) with Jesus describing those who stand with him. They may not be his blood relations—his mother and brothers—but those around him, his true disciples, form a new family created out of obedience and trust in him.

Since there is such heterogeneity in this lesson, the preacher may move in many different directions. Placed in juxtaposition with the First Lesson, the emphasis in the passage upon Jesus' confrontation with those forces enslaving or distorting humanity shows his intention to overcome the division so vividly dramatized in Genesis 3. A complementary move would be to center attention upon this new family being created in Christ, to establish new relationships in contrast with the broken relationships evident in the human scene.

The Fourth Sunday after Pentecost

Lutheran	Roman Catholic	Episcopal	Pres/UCC/Chr	Meth/COCU
Ezek. 17:22–24	Ezek. 17:22–24	Ezek. 31:1–6, 10–14	Ezek. 17:22–24	Ezek. 17:22–24
2 Cor. 5:1–10	2 Cor. 5:6–10	2 Cor. 5:1–10	2 Cor. 5:6–10	2 Cor. 5:1–10
Mark 4:26–34	Mark 4:26–34	Mark 4:26–34	Mark 4:26–34	Mark 4:26–34

EXEGESIS

First Lesson: Ezek. 17:22–24. This passage celebrates the hope for the nation's restoration and eschatological magnificence. Its real point, however, emerges only in light of the entire chapter. Vv. 1–10 (the allegory of two eagles) interpret Judah's historical experience: the first eagle (Nebuchadrezzar) carries off the top of the cedar (the Davidic head of state in Jerusalem) into Babylonian exile. The "seed of the land" and what it becomes is the puppet-king Zedekiah, whose rule depends on Babylonian hegemony. The second eagle (Egypt) lures him into rebellion against Babylon, a futile move. Vv. 11–21 interpret the allegory. Over against that, our text (vv. 22–24) portrays God's own action: God too will take the top of the cedar (a mere sprig, a tender twig) and will plant it on the height in the holy land, where it will become a great cedar, providing shelter for all sorts of beasts and birds. All other trees (nations) will know that it is God who is at work in the rise and fall of nations (see also Isa. 41:17–20). The theme of eschatological inversion (or reversal) appears also in the teaching of Jesus (for example, Matt. 5:5; 10:30; Luke 14:7–11).

The great tree is a widespread symbol of life (as in Eden) and/or of power (for example, Judg. 9:7–15; 1 Kings 6:35). It is not surprising to find it used to image national glory. Ezekiel 31 uses the tree, in a negative sense, to represent Egypt, as Daniel 4 does with Babylon. Its shading and sheltering roles (17:23; 31:6 [note the reversal in vv. 12–13]; Dan. 4:12) suggest the beneficent character of power. The gigantic size of the trees picks up an element of the mythical "world tree," the tree of life.

Second Lesson: 2 Cor. 5:1–10. This lesson continues the discussion from which last Sunday's reading was taken. Even though the imagery shifts to "tent," and then to "garment," the subject matter explicates the "eternal weight of glory" (4:17), what Paul elsewhere calls the "spiritual body" (1 Cor. 15:50). The rhetorical contrasts (see comment on 2 Cor. 4:13–18) are continued: earthly/heavenly; handmade/not made by hands. Paul shares with most antiquity the assumption—which is the opposite of the one widely held today—that what is invisible (4:18) and heavenly (5:3–4) is more real than that which is visible and earthly. Therefore, he can long for the unseen mode of existence.

In 5:1–5 Paul seems to struggle to say what he means and to avoid saying what he does not mean. He affirms the superiority of the future mode of existence; yet he does not want to say categorically that the transition from the present to the future is by way of a naked soul, stripped of body. That would express too much antipathy toward the body. So he points out that he does not expect to be "unclothed" (the soul stripped of body) but he expects to be "further clothed." (NEB is apt: "we do not want to have the old body stripped off . . . [but] to have the new body put on over it.'') Not release *from* body but redemption *of* body by transformation (Rom. 8:23) is the Christian hope. The presence of the Spirit is for Paul the "down payment" (RSV's "guarantee" is misleading; KJV's "earnest money" is apt), a first fruits of the impending harvest, because the new moral life made possible by the Spirit (Rom. 8:2–4; Gal. 5:22–24) betokens the deeper transformation to come.

Chap. 5:6–10 continues the content but shifts the imagery to "being at home/being away." It should not be pressed, for Paul clearly implies that the Lord is with the believer; indeed, the believer is "in Christ." In v. 9 Paul relativizes the importance of the contrast. V. 10 emphasizes accountability for what one has done as a phenomenal, psychosomatic body-self. Body is not only physical matter; it is morally significant as the expression of the self.

Gospel: Mark 4:26–34. This lesson consists of two seed parables (the first found only in Mark, the second also in Matt. 13:31–32; Luke 13:18–19) followed by a summary comment on all the parables in the chapter. The conclusion should not be taken literally, for even in Mark there are other forms of teaching. Mark implies that as a whole Jesus' teaching has a "parabolic" quality: its meaning is not self-evident to all but requires explanation as in vv. 13–20.

Parables are not illustrations of a moral which can be stated independently; they are narrative metaphors in which the configuration of the plot suggests, invites, teases the hearer to regard a certain reality in an unconventional way. If a parable "works," the hearer "gets it" the way one "gets" a joke. Mark clearly regards parables somewhat differently—as containing deep truth which must be brought to the surface. Perhaps he understood them this way because his context was basically different from that of Jesus.

The first parable uses the mystery of growth to suggest how it is with regard to the kingdom. It has its own inner dynamic which leads from seeding to harvesting. The interpreter is easily lured into allegorizing each element of the parable: the sower, the seed, growth by stages, the harvest. This might be how Mark understood it, but this is true neither to the nature of parable nor to the way Jesus probably used parables.

The second parable is something of a takeoff on the tradition of the symbolic trees noted in our OT lesson. (Here too the nesting birds appear.) But now the image of power is transformed: the giant tree is but a giant shrub. The point shifts from the transplanting of a tree's top to a tiny mustard seed which becomes large. Moreover, it is no longer the kingdom of earthly potentates or nationalism that is expected, but the sovereignty of God. There is nothing "Davidic" about the mustard bush! In a way, this parable is a critique of what is expressed in Ezek. 17:22–24.

HOMILETICAL INTERPRETATION

First Lesson: Ezek. 17:22–24. This passage, to be understood, must be set against the backdrop of Judah's history as told in the allegory of the eagles in the first part of chap. 17. The situation for Judah appears hopeless. Crushed by Babylonian arms, with king and leaders deported to Babylon, Judah's futile rebellion against Babylon, in league with Egypt, has simply tightened the noose around its neck. Judah's recent past is marked with tragedies, its future is bleak. All the evidences of history point toward the end of all its hopes and dreams. Against this hopeless backdrop the passage of hope is written. Yahweh now enters. He will take a tender shoot and place it upon Mount Zion; there it will grow into a great tree large enough to give shelter to birds from near and far. This act of Yahweh leads to the central affirmation of the passage that the key to history is not held by world powers such as Babylon or Egypt. God is the one who decides the fate of the nations of the earth, bringing low the mighty tree and exalting the lowly.

The relevance of the passage is immediately apparent to us, living as we do with the constant panorama of nation vying with nation for supremacy, each seeking power and prestige. The determining factor for world supremacy seems to be the nuclear stockpile; the nation possessing nuclear superiority holds the key to the future. Thus does modern humanity assign the lordship of history. This passage turns that all around. The key to the future lies in the hands of God, who works with a different set of criteria, who chooses not the mighty nor the powerful but the seemingly weak and the lowly. The passage then is a message of hope, affirming that God's purposes ultimately are being achieved, despite all evidences to the contrary. It is also a reminder that God's purposes are achieved through the most unlikely, the most insignificant factors, totally reversing expectations. The passage thus anticipates the NT emphasis upon the way God brings low the mighty and exalts the humble (cf. Luke 1:52) and chooses what is weak in the world to shame the strong (1 Cor. 1:27). The passage is then a reminder lest we become captured by worldly standards of size, power, and prestige and fail to see God's power at work in the seemingly insignificant, often overlooked, areas of human life. As we shall see, this will have impact upon the Marcan passage for this Sunday.

Second Lesson: 2 Cor. 5:1–10. As has been seen from last Sunday's passage, Paul is dealing, in this section of the Corinthian letter, with the Christian's confrontation with death. While Paul may have thought earlier that he would live to the Parousia, it is as if now he faces with other Christians the reality of death, and he speaks to it both for himself and for others. His words speak forcefully over the centuries to our culture with its denial of death and silence in the face of it. Most of us are aware of the studies of Elisabeth Kübler-Ross and her findings about the loneliness of dying and the failure of chaplains, pastors, and counselors to express any faith or ideas about this, the universal "passage" in life. These words of Paul fill a tragic vacuum now evident in the modern Christian church.

Paul first (in 5:1–5) affirms the inadequacy and the transitory nature of the present life when compared to what God has prepared. He uses the image of the tent to convey what our present life is like. A tent—as Paul, a maker of tents, well knew—is temporary. It is portable, made to be conveyed from place to place; no place is a fixed dwelling place. But God has prepared a house for us, not temporary, not destructible, where we may finally be "at home." Paul sees the present dimension of existence as touched with anxiety, but the future dimension will swallow up the present in eternal life. Paul guards against the dichotomy of body/spirit by using the image of being further clothed: we are not destroyed; there is a continuity between what is now and what shall be. The Christian knows something of the reality of this future transformation by the gift of the Spirit, which is a pledge or guarantee of what shall be.

Paul, after speaking of the inadequacy of the present life in 5:6–10, speaks of the source of courage for the Christian in facing death. There are many kinds of courage at a time of death: a courage of despair, recognizing the inevitability of it all; a stoic courage, desiring even at the last to play it out well. Commendable as these may be, they are quite unlike the courage expressed here, a courage based upon hope. Paul does not see the issue of life and death as that of being or nonbeing. He sees a consistency running through life into death, a consistency of being "with Christ." One is reminded here of Rom. 8:38ff., of the constancy of the love of God in Christ. Paul is silent about what lies beyond the present life except to insist that Christ will be there; therefore he can make that most incredible of statements, "We would rather be away from the body and at home with the Lord."

The modern American interpreter faces a dilemma unknown to Paul. The people of Paul's day most certainly felt their daily existence a burden to be borne. But the modern American Christian finds very little discomfort in the present materialistic life. The transitory inadequacy of life in the tent imagery will have to be dealt with by reflecting upon the complex inadequacies of our existence—our fears, our insecurities, and our anxieties. It is in the presence of these that there is a fuller, transformed life we long to experience and have experienced as an intimation in the gift of the Spirit.

Gospel: Mark 4:26–34. These two parables are set in the context of Jesus' struggle against opposition. They have been a comfort to the church down through the centuries whenever the church has seemed insignificant, its promises unfulfilled, its hope futile.

The first parable, that of the seed growing secretly, holds before the listener the image of a seed sown in a field, unattended, nothing seemingly taking place. But mysteriously, the seed is growing and will eventually produce fruit. To the early struggling disciple band, to the primitive church, to the church of today—the story affirms that the growth of the kingdom is certain, though hidden and gradual. Significant is the fact that no emphasis is placed upon a farmer in the field, preparing the soil or uprooting weeds. What is being said is that human effort and industry do not insure the breaking in and growth of the kingdom. The process of God's will developing in the world continues simply because it is God's intention. Hidden it may be, at times imperceptible in its growth, until observers may even exclaim, "Nothing is happening!"—but the process has been set in motion, and its outcome is sure.

Assuredly this is not counsel for us to do nothing; commitment never knows the alternative of inactivity. Assuredly it is counsel (and a note of grace) for us to be willing to wait in absolute confidence and assurance in the outcome, to endure times when nothing seems to be happening, knowing that the issue rests in the hands of God.

The second parable, that of the mustard seed, emphasizes the fact that small beginnings need not indicate insignificant results. The insignificant mustard seed flowers into a bush providing shade for "the birds of the air." Little imagination is needed to grasp how this parable spoke to the needs of the small mustard-seed fellowship of the early church existing in the shadow of world powers. It is an affirmation echoing both in imagery and in content something of Ezekiel 17. God works his purposes out through the insignificant; the small beginnings of the kingdom in obscure Palestine will one day embrace everything. For them it was only a promise and a hope unrealized, but we have seen some indication of its truth, of a gospel that does reach out now to embrace the world. And yet, despite our recognition of this truth, we are victimized by bigness. The size of a church and the prestige of a pulpit (the statistical indexes of success) are equated with the kingdom. Could it still not be that the power of the kingdom may begin and be present in unobtrusive places, unknown and unrecognized?

The Fifth Sunday after Pentecost

Lutheran	Roman Catholic	Episcopal	Pres/UCC/Chr	Meth/COCU
Job 38:1–11	Job 38:1, 8–11	Job 38:1–11, 16–18	Job 38:1–11	Job 38:1–11, 16–18
2 Cor. 5:14–21	2 Cor. 5:14–17	2 Cor. 5:14–21	2 Cor. 5:16–21	2 Cor. 5:14–21
Mark 4:35–41	Mark 4:35–41	Mark 4:35–41; (5:1–20)	Mark 4:35–41	Mark 4:35–5:20

EXEGESIS

First Lesson: Job 38:1–11, 16–18. With this passage God the inscrutable steps out of silence to confront Job. In chap. 31, Job had asserted his moral rectitude, in the course of which he challenged God, "Let the Almighty answer me" (31:35). Before God responds, however, Elihu tries his hand at setting Job straight (chaps. 32—37). God's response comes in two cycles: (1) chaps. 38—39 emphasize God's mastery of what we call "nature," and in chap. 40:1–2 God challenges Job, who is impressed enough to be silenced but not persuaded; (2) the passage 40:6—41:39 emphasizes God's sovereignty over the monsters of chaos, Behemoth and Leviathan.

Both cycles begin with God's identical challenge to Job except that the first is introduced by a contemptuous question (compare 38:2–3 and 40:6–7). Its function is to put distance between Job and the reader, who up to this point has probably identified with Job; now, however, the reader learns that God regards the hero as a man who speaks passionately but out of ignorance. Like 40:7, 38:3 also makes the point that now it is God who asks the questions, and he expects an answer. The first answer (40:3–5) shows that Job is overwhelmed; the second (42:1–6) takes up 38:2–3 and 40:6–7.

By omitting 38:12–15, our lesson calls attention first to God the

Creator, then to his divine sovereignty over the sea. However, this obscures the pattern of the whole chapter, which moves back and forth between heaven and earth (all the created order): 8–11, sea; 11–15, sky; 16–18, sea; 19–21, sky; 22–30, earth (snow, rain, ice); and 31–38, sky.

Two things should be noted. (1) Our lesson, like all of God's words to Job, celebrates the divine sovereignty and mystery, in light of which human knowledge appears rather puny. This is a magnificent poetic celebration of God the Creator. It can stand alone; it does not require its present context in the Book of Job to be intelligible. (2) But in the book, the passage *is* God's "answer" to Job's question. Yet it is not an answer, not an explanation at all. Rather, it is a response which puts Job's question into perspective; it is not an answer Job expected. In fact, one must decide whether this is a put-down, designed to make Job wish he had never demanded a reckoning from God, or whether this is actually a profound answer, on another level, to Job's question.

Second Lesson: 2 Cor. 5:14–21. The omitted verses (vv. 11–13) link this reading with that of last Sunday and show that Paul is still interpreting himself as an emissary of Christ (the theme continues beyond our lesson; see 6:1–10). The context shows that "the love of Christ" (v. 14) refers to Christ's love, not ours for him. The latter part of v. 14 appears to be a christological formula, from which v. 15 draws the pertinent conclusion. When Paul undertakes his apostolic labor, marked by difficulties of all sorts (for example, 4:7–12; 6:3–10), he understands himself to be acting for the sake of Christ; Paul must represent him in a way that is appropriate to the Christ-event. Yet this is not peculiar to Paul; rather it is constitutive of *Christian* existence, as v. 15 makes clear. Paul's self-interpretation is paradigmatic, not exemplary. A paradigm, through a particular instance, exposes the structure of what *is* generally true; an example, however, is something that *ought to become* true of another particular.

Vv. 16–21 constitute a highly compressed paragraph in which fundamental themes of Paul's thought flow into one another: in Christ, new creation, reconciliation, God's righteousness (implying God's rectifying work, Rom. 3:21–26), and the "incarnation"—a word Paul does not use. V. 16 contains an exegetical problem which the RSV solves (more or less correctly): literally the Greek reads, "even if we knew according to flesh Christ." Does "according to flesh" modify Christ (thus implying that Paul is not interested in a fleshly, phenomenal, historical Jesus, as has been claimed), or does it go with "knew" (thus referring to a way of knowing, which Paul makes clear by applying it even to Jesus)? Doubtless the latter is correct. From the standpoint of being "in Christ" (living in the sphere of his lordship) and of sharing in new creation, the Christian is no longer to regard anyone in a fleshly way. If surface appearances are no longer decisive, then one no longer is impressed by signs of power or prowess, no longer esteems a person on the basis of manifest worth or moral achievement. God does not "count" trespasses against a person (he does not relate to a person on the basis of rule keeping)—that is what reconciliation, initiated by God, entails.

V. 19 probably should be translated "in Christ God was reconciling" because the point concerns what God was doing through Christ, not where God was while reconciliation was occurring. Just as v. 14 grounds Christian self-understanding in the Christ-event, so v. 21 gives the christological basis for v. 20. The sinless, preexistent One was made what we are (existence marked by sin) so that we can become what he is—the manifestation of God's rectitude (through reconciliation).

The ministry of reconciliation is, therefore, first of all the word of God's deed. As God acted through Christ, so God acts through the word and work of the ambassador (v. 20), whose existence in the world is consonant with the Christ-event.

Gospel: Mark 4:35–41. (See Matt. 8:23–27; Luke 8:22–25.) This remarkable story tempts the interpreter to misplace the emphasis. On the one hand, even conservative commentators call attention to the fact that storms develop and abate suddenly on this lake, as if this "natural" explanation illumined the story's point. (Surely the fishermen knew the weather patterns as well as an inland carpenter!) So the story is not about the miraculous coincidence of Jesus' word and the sudden calm. It is about Jesus' authority to cause the calm by his command. On the other hand, the story does not urge faith based on the miraculous, for although Jesus' uncanny power prompts the disciples to respond appropriately with fear (RSV: "awe"), it does not elicit a confession of faith. In fact, Mark emphasizes the incapacity of the miraculous to do so (see 6:45–52; 8:14–21). So the story should not be interpreted to mean that Jesus' mighty power shows adequately who he is. From Mark's point of view that is possible only if one already knows who Jesus is (on the basis of resurrection); the occurrence of a miracle only poses the question, as v. 41 shows.

A story like this is evocative and suggestive; it appeals to the imagination, and its language resonates with more than one OT text, including today's lesson (see also Ps. 89:9; 107:28–29; Jonah 1, for example). V. 39 uses the same verbs as 1:25, where the demonic is silenced (also 9:25).

Note that the disciples' question in v. 38 is a tacit rebuke of Jesus for sleeping (a detail which Matthew and Luke change). Note also that in Mark, Jesus rebukes the disciples after the calm appears, so that it seems as if the disciples' awe comes as a response to his word; Matthew and Luke reverse the sequence, so that the disciples' awe is a response to the miracle.

In Mark the real climax of the story is the disparity between Jesus' word and that of the disciples. Jesus' words are transmitted in various ways in the textual tradition; the main alternatives are (1) "Why are you afraid? Do you not yet have faith?" and (2) "Why are you so afraid? Why do you not have faith?" The latter asks for an explanation; the former is preferred. The disciples did, of course, have a certain "faith," or else they would not have awakened Jesus. Yet this is not deemed real faith, perhaps because anxiety-impelled faith which turns people to Jesus for deliverance in emergencies is not the faith Jesus calls for.

HOMILETICAL INTERPRETATION

First Lesson: Job 38:1–11, 16–18. This passage may somewhat bemuse the preacher and make him or her wonder about those selecting lectionary passages. For while it is evident that the passage does produce some background material for the Gospel this week by affirming God's sovereignty over all creation, even the sea, it is evident also that the selection dips awkwardly into the midst of what is surely one of the most magnificent presentations of humanity's search for ultimate answers in the face of life's tragedies. The exegesis is correct that the passage on creation may stand alone. It does speak of the power of the Creator to set limits even on the seas, which for the Hebrews were the symbol of mysterious, dark, and uncontrollable forces. But the interpreter may feel uneasy treating a peripheral portion of this "answer" to Job's question and may therefore understandably be led to put aside other considerations and be caught up in the grandeur of this passage.

The issue is universal—how to make sense of the meaninglessness of life with its evil and suffering cutting across our best efforts. The question broods in the heart of every sensitive person and finds expression in Job's search for the answer. Verse by verse, chapter by chapter, the orthodox answers are furnished Job by his friends, but they answer nothing. Then finally the dialogue between Job and his friends ends with the words, "then the Lord answered. . . ." One waits now at long last for the "answer," but nothing new is added. Though the chapter is expressed in magnificent poetry, everything said has been said or is known. God appears, and what he says changes nothing, and yet in reality everything is changed. One then is placed before the more profound "answer." The answer is not instruction about creation but is the presence of God. The Christian interpreter feels a depth here not realized by the author of Job. Human suffering and tragedy do not yield to syllogism or reason for answers, but the Presence and faith in the One taking upon himself our humanity and becoming involved in the midst of tragedy in the cross speaks the clearest word. A sermon touching or elaborating on this strikes a responsive chord in every heart. Modern society exists in the midst of an escalation of factual knowledge but still stands perplexed before Job's ancient question.

Second Lesson: 2 Cor. 5:14–21. The interpreter is confronted with an embarrassment of riches in this passage. As the exegesis points out, "fundamental themes of Paul's thought flow into one another," and the preacher is placed before a banquet of sermon possibilities. But to realize them, the minister needs to grasp that while Paul continues to defend his ministry, by describing his experience he provides at the same time a pattern for all Christians and not just for professional ministers.

First, the passage speaks of the motivation for the Christian life—the love of Christ. The compelling force issues forth from what Christ has done in the cross, demonstrating the breadth and depth of his love for all. This love of Christ acts as the impelling, controlling force for Paul, not because it is just for him, but because of its vastness for all humanity. This results in a changing of the way Paul looks at his fellow human beings. No longer does he look upon persons and value them by usual standards of material possessions or influence, or the lack of them. Now the determining factor is that this person is "one for whom Christ died" (John Calvin).

Second, the passage speaks of the transforming power of Christ's love. To express the power of this experience, Paul uses the image of a new creation, of the old age passing away and of a new age coming. Whether the metaphor is that of a new birth or of a new creation, it is an attempt to express the dramatic change occurring within the Christian's life. There is a shifting of the center of existence. Instead of being self-centered, life now centers "in Christ." But the preacher/interpreter must be careful lest the impression be given that this event comes only in a moment. Assuredly, Paul telescopes the experience, for he had before him the stumbling Corinthian Christians, who had made a start but were far from being a finished product. Nevertheless, despite all their inadequacies, despite all external evidence to the contrary, a new thing has begun in them.

Third, the passage speaks of God's intention in Christ, and how this is also our ministry. This intention is caught in the phrase, "in Christ God was reconciling the world to himself." The love which compels us in ministry is that love which identifies itself with our brokenness so that we may be healed and restored to God. It is instructive that in the late sixties a mainline denomination writing a new confessional document chose reconciliation as its central theme. The preface of the document states: "God's reconciling work in Jesus Christ, and the mission of reconciliation to which is called his church are the heart of the gospel in any age" (The Confession of 1967, United Presbyterian Church U.S.A.).

Gospel: Mark 4:35–41. The dramatic vividness of this story of the storm should remind the preacher both of the power of narrative to arrest attention and the inseparableness of form and content. Much of what is affirmed here loses something of its force if it is separated from the story of the storm and turned into propositional truths. The preacher, then, should utilize creative imagination in preaching the sermon.

The story focuses on the responses and faith of the disciples; sermons might be formed with differing emphases.

One might highlight the question "Who then is this?" This question is posed at the conclusion, after the power of Jesus' words calms the turbulent waters. The interpreter must be aware here that in Hebrew thought the chaotic, mysterious sea was greatly feared and considered to be beyond the power of anyone other than God. Creation is described in terms of a struggle between God and the sea; God alone has power to confine the sea: "Thus far shall you come, and no farther" (Job 38:11). Jesus' authority and power over the waters raises again the question repeated throughout this Gospel about his identity. "Who then is this?" is the suitable question for the disciples, and it is still *the* question for those of us being confronted by him. Without hesitation, modern persons call Jesus "teacher," placing him as one among many wise persons who have arrested the attention of humanity. But the story challenges the adequacy of such answers, pressing the reader to look again at the figure of the Nazarene.

A second way for the passage to be handled would be to underscore what is perhaps its central emphasis—the response of the disciples' faith. One needs to be reminded that in Mark the twelve disciples do not represent a paradigm of faithfulness and commitment. They are as we are—blind to who Jesus is and consistently inadequate in their responses to him. Here, in this story, it is not that they lack all faith; they turn to Jesus to be rescued. Their failure is the inadequacy of their faith to stand against the testing of the storm. There is a kind of faith, a knee-jerk response in time of physical danger or crisis, that prays and calls for deliverance. One should not ridicule such faith, but what Jesus seeks is a faith that denies self, even in the face of the cross.

The Sixth Sunday after Pentecost

Lutheran	Roman Catholic	Episcopal	PresUCC/Chr	Meth/COCU
Lam. 3:22–33	Wisd. 1:13–15; 2:23–24	Deut. 15:7–11	Gen. 4:3–10	Lam. 3:22–33 or Wisd. 1:13–15; 2:23–24
2 Cor. 8:1–9, 13–14	2 Cor. 8:7–9, 13–15	2 Cor. 8:1–9, 13–15	2 Cor. 8:7–15	2 Cor. 8:1–15
Mark 5:21–24a, 35–43 or Mark 5:24b–34	Mark 5:21–43 or Mark 5:21–24, 35b–43	Mark 5:22–24, 35b–43	Mark 5:21–43	Mark 5:21–43

EXEGESIS

First Lesson: Lam. 3:22–33. These affirmative thoughts, which are actually introduced in v. 21, strike the only positive note in the entire chapter. To be true to the pericope and its function, the interpreter needs to see its role as the counterpoint to the rest of the chapter.

Lamentations 3 (like chaps. 1, 2, 4) is an acrostic poem, whose lines begin with the first, second, third, etc., letter of the Hebrew alphabet. In this chapter, however, the author produces a tour de force—the same letter begins each line of a three-line strophe. This artistry is lost in translation. More important, unlike any other chapter, this chapter emphasizes the "I" (and in some places "we"). The "I" begins our passage (v. 21), but in v. 25 the style changes to generalizing statements without personal reference. No one knows who the "I" is. Since the tradition that it is Jeremiah has been given up, it is likely that this is a stylistic "I": the suffering of an individual has been made representative of anyone who feels opposed by God (3:1–20). The phrases used to describe this suffering echo those of the lament psalms and of Job as well. Whether chap. 3 reflects the agony caused by the destruction of Jerusalem, as does the rest of the book, is not clear.

Over against the Job-like indictment of God in vv. 1–20, our lesson celebrates God's steadfast love (*hesed*). How can both themes be expressed side by side? There are two clues: (1) according to vv. 31–33, God's hostility is temporary, moderated by compassion, and reluctant (literally "not from the heart"—God's "heart is not in it"); (2) according to v. 38, both good and evil come from God (see also Isa. 45:7, Amos 3:6). Where there is no "Satan," monotheism has always had to struggle with this theme.

If vv. 22–23 are read with v. 21, then it is fairly clear that these verses expose a particular function for theological insight. That is, vv. 22–33 celebrate God's fidelity and goodness and also acknowledge—to the point of obsequiousness—humility before God (vv. 28–30). These are classical theological affirmations of Hebrew faith. In rehearsing them, in affirming them, in calling them to mind in the midst of despair, the suffering person has a glimmer of hope, because one tacitly acknowledges that one's own experience of God is not the only truth about God.

Second Lesson: 2 Cor. 8:1–15. In the midst of 2 Corinthians the reader comes upon two chapters that deal with the collection of funds for the poor Christians in Jerusalem (chaps. 8—9); they seem to have been written on different occasions. At the Council of Jerusalem, Paul had agreed to collect this money (Gal. 2:10), for he regarded it as an important symbol of the unity of the church: gentile Christians should contribute to the needs of their Jewish brothers and sisters. In 1 Cor. 16:1–2 he specified how the money should be gathered. After the collection was complete, Paul decided to take it personally to Jerusalem (Rom. 15:24–29). Acts is silent about this fund, except for the odd reference to "alms and offerings" which Paul brought "to my nation" (24:17)—as if the money were to be deposited in the temple. 2 Corinthians 8 was apparently carried by Titus to Corinth; our 2 Corinthians gathers up various letters to Corinth, chaps. 8 and 9 among them.

Paul tells the Corinthians that the Macedonians (Christians in Philippi, Thessalonica, and elsewhere) were generous despite their poverty; indeed, they insisted on participating, having first committed themselves "to the Lord and to us by the will of God" (v. 5). With this precedent in view, the Corinthians are to be as outstanding in their giving as they are in faith, speech, knowledge, seriousness, and love for Paul (v. 7). But the really important precedent is christological—the incarnation (v. 9 does not refer to the self-impoverishment of the carpenter from Nazareth but the self-abasement of God's Son). Then Paul adduces a third consideration: one's contribution is to be measured (and legitimated) not by what one is unable to give but by what one can give (v. 12). In vv. 13–14 Paul appears to be answering the objection, "If we give generously, they will not need to work." He responds by writing about a "parity" (RSV: "equality"): "you give of your abundance to meet their [financial] need; their [spiritual] abundance meets your [spiritual] need"—that is, the gospel you received stems ultimately from Jerusalem. V. 15 applies Exod. 16:18 to the present situation. Exodus reports that when the Israelites gathered manna, some gathered much, some little; yet when it was measured, each had just enough. He who gathered much had no excess, and he who gathered little had no lack. In Paul's hands, the line from Exodus refers not to gathering but to giving. The main point, however, is the same—by sharing, everyone's supply is equalized. Paul does not mention, here or elsewhere, the "sharing of goods," which Acts reports (2:44–46; 4:34–35), but what he writes about the offering (see also Rom. 15:24–29) seems to be in the spirit of that initial "experiment."

Gospel: Mark 5:21–43. (See Matt. 9:18–26 [abbreviated]; Luke 8:40–56.) One feature of this pericope is the fact that it concerns Jesus' wonderous power with respect to women; another feature is the Marcan device of using one story as the setting, the "framework," for another (that is, 6:6–13, 30 frames 6:17–29; 11:12–14, 20–25 frames 11:15–19; 14:53–54, 66–72 frames 14:55–65); yet another feature is that both stories deal with faith (vv. 34, 36).

The fact that we learn the father's name but not that of the girl confirms that Jairus was a leading citizen; the story is less interested in the girl (not because she was a girl) than in the father, because, in the nature of the case, only he could have faith. The story assumes that this official believes in Jesus to the extent that he thinks Jesus can spare his daughter from death—a point Jesus does not contest. When news of the girl's death reaches the party, Jesus is undeterred (v. 36). Instead, Jesus addresses Jairus in words associated with theophanies: "Fear not!" Then he summons the father to faith—from Mark's view, a more adequate faith is possible only as a "nevertheless" (one is reminded of Paul's explication of Abrahamic faith in Romans 4). We are not told why only the inner circle of disciples is permitted to accompany Jesus and Jairus; perhaps Mark regards what is about to happen as a prefiguration of the resurrection. V. 38 reflects custom; the report of the mourning heightens the dramatic power of the story—everybody knows the girl is dead. Jesus, however, declares that she is "sleeping"—then as now a metaphor for death, but one which suggests that waking will follow. Then, with parents and disciples as witnesses, he revives her. The English, like the Greek, has preserved the Aramaic, because it was regarded as a word of power—though clearly it was not a magical incantation. This story should not be regarded as a resurrection story, for the girl is merely restored to life, resuscitated. The story assumes that, like Lazarus (John 11), she will die later. Resurrection, on the other hand, is transformation into deathlessness. V. 43 states one of Mark's themes: secrecy. Matthew omitted it and, instead, drew the obvious conclusion: the story spread (Matt. 9:26). Was Mark naive? Not really. He does not say that the secret was kept. The function of the command is to suggest that not until Jesus' resurrection can one know properly that Jesus is the one who conquered death.

The woman with an unhealable hemorrhage is another instance of faith as confidence in Jesus the wonderworker. In fact, her belief verges on superstition—the belief that mere contact with things that touch Jesus is enough to heal. And it worked! (See also Acts 19:11–12.) Moreover, those who told and retold this story shared her belief, for they reported that Jesus felt power being drained from him. Such reports from other healers are also known. Perhaps Jesus too understood it this way, though this report is unique. But the main point is what happens next. Jesus shifts the emphasis from the flow of power from him to the flow of faith from her and declares that her faith "saved" her (RSV's "has made you well" is too restrictive; the word means both healing and salvation in the extended sense). Jesus did not reject her crude view of faith—confidence in the power of a wonderworker—but accepted it as a valid form of faith in *her* situation. Neither in the case of Jairus nor in this case did Jesus first correct their view of faith before he responded. In both cases, however, he tacitly deepened their faith.

HOMILETICAL INTERPRETATION

First Lesson: Lam. 3:22–33. In this passage, the author searches for some steadying center in life in the face of overwhelming tragedy. This material was written in the midst of political and religious crises. The person who wrote these poems had been brought up to believe that his nation, Judah, had been blessed by God; the land was a gift from God, and the temple to his God in Jerusalem was the center of the universe. But the land and people have suffered irretrievable calamity. The armies of Babylon have swept across the land. The once vaunted national hope is destroyed. The land and temple are in ruins; the people are in exile thousands of miles away across a trackless desert. The poem is a search for something in life, amid all of life's tragedies, that will remain certain and sure when all else has been swept away. The interpreter, understanding the dimension of tragedy behind these words, feels a certain kinship. While he or she may not see in the modern national scene the same profile of tragedy, there are too evident in many individual lives crushed hopes and dreams, sudden illnesses and deaths, that sweep away all our visible means of support, challenging both pew and pulpit to seek for something steady in the earthquakes of daily life.

The poem affirms for its answer, as must the sermon, one of the great words of OT faith, *hesed,* translated "steadfast love." It is the sure, steady love of God for his people, expressed at the heart of the covenant and maintained by God independent of humankind's response. The poem affirms that, despite all external evidences to the contrary, God's faithfulness is sure, "his mercies never come to an end." This steadfast love, focused in the OT in the Covenant at Sinai, is for the Christian interpreter refocused in the NT in the life, death, and resurrection of Jesus Christ and in the New Covenant. The steadfast love is the love of God in Jesus Christ pledged to us not because of who we are and what we do but because of who God is and his faithfulness to us. To be able to affirm this steadfast love, that it is renewed every morning, that it is a certainty in the midst of life, provides for the minister an opportunity to speak to many troubled lives.

Second Lesson: 2 Cor. 8:1–15. Paul addresses here a particular problem about raising a fund for the poor Christians in Jerusalem. Its importance for the minister is what Paul is saying generally about Christian giving. How many ministers are called upon to speak on giving during stewardship seasons or for some worthy cause and either feel inadequate or demeaned by it? How instructive and helpful is this passage, for it places generosity in a responsible theological context and lifts it up as an essential part of the Christian life. Here, as elsewhere in his correspondence to the early churches, Paul never hesitated to speak about giving as part of the Christian life. As one reflects on this material, several insights emerge about Christians' generosity, any one or combination of which might provide a basis for a sermon.

Christian generosity is a result of a committed Christian life. Paul, in describing the outstanding liberality of the poverty-stricken Macedonian church, writes, ". . . but first they gave themselves to the Lord." So long as we stand at the center of life, our needs take priority and the grace of liberality is stifled. It is when we consecrate our life to the Lord that we are freed from our possessions so that they may be used by him. Our means follow our heart's commitment.

Christian generosity is motivated by the model of Christ. To determine how we are to respond, we are to look at the grace of our Lord Jesus Christ: "though he was rich, yet for our sakes he became poor." It is God's love and willingness to take upon himself (in Christ) the form of a servant that enables us, in response, to give of ourselves. Grace precedes generosity, awakening in the heart a sense of gratitude. A great many campaigns for funds in churches try to motivate people to give by comparing them to other church members. Our self-image, our pride, our community prestige are made the motivating factors. How differently Paul speaks, pointing to Christ.

Christian generosity contributes to the unity of the church. Paul's eagerness for the Corinthian Christians to give to the poor in Jerusalem is certainly based upon the need of the church. But there is also the awareness of how such giving witnesses to the interdependence of Christians with one another. One may be able to give material necessities, but the other may give spiritual insights; each has something the other needs. In our century we may be rediscovering this truth; Western, affluent churches who sent money for missions are now receiving back from Third World countries new perspectives on the Christian faith that challenge, sustain, and minister to us.

Gospel: Mark 5:21–43. The preacher is confronted in this passage with two basic problems of approaching the material: first, how to deal with the Marcan characteristic of telescoping two narratives into one piece; and second, how to prevent attention from being diverted from the major thrust of the passages to the elements of the miraculous.

The first problem demands attention simply because one knows how difficult it is for a congregation to focus upon more than one theme or idea. The answer may be for the interpreter to seek for the unifying factor in the two vignettes—in this case, the issue of faith—and to allow that to keep the material united.

The second problem is much more difficult; it is how to center attention upon the faith question rather than upon the miraculous touch or the raising from the dead. The modern listener likely is more concerned about whether the story is true than about its meaning. Perhaps the best approach for the preacher wishing to emphasize the central theme of faith is simply to point out that we often ask misleading questions about biblical stories and thus miss their central word to us—in this case, the question of faith.

Faith is a dominant concern of Mark, and in these two portraits of Jairus and the unknown woman there emerge new understandings of faith.

In the case of Jairus, faith is absolute trust and confidence in Jesus. This, the story affirms, is enough. The threat to this faith comes to Jairus at the news of his daughter's death. At that point human judgment would have been to give up in the face of reality. But Jesus' words, "Do not fear, only believe," are the affirmation of the need for confident faith even in the face of the reality of death. A central attribute of faith is this radical trust, even when the "evidence" seems to contradict our expectations. This radical trust is the way to the "saving" of the young child. In the story of the unknown woman, faith again is the condition of being healed. Here, however, there is a sensitive insight in the progression of a tentative faith into a deepening understanding. The woman sees in Jesus the miracle worker whose power flows even through his garment. There is no rebuke of this rather superstitious faith. She was wrong about the power of the garment; she was right in her confidence in Jesus. The words of Jesus, "Your faith has made you well," affirm that it is always faith that saves.

Both of these vignettes hold before us the affirmation that healing and salvation come through the commitment of life to God in Jesus Christ. This radical trust in him wins through, despite the reality of death and the distortion of faith by superstition.

The Seventh Sunday after Pentecost

Lutheran	Roman Catholic	Episcopal	Pres/UCC/Chr	Meth/COCU
Ezek. 2:1–5	Ezek. 2:2–5	Ezek. 2:1–7	Ezek. 2:1–5	Ezek. 2:1–7
2 Cor. 12:7–10	2 Cor. 12:7–10	2 Cor. 12:2–10	2 Cor. 12:7–10	2 Cor. 12:7–10
Mark 6:1–6	Mark 6:1–6	Mark 6:1–6	Mark 6:1–6	Mark 6:1–6

EXEGESIS

First Lesson: Ezek. 2:1-7. This pericope inaugurates a series of commissionings (chaps. 2—3) which follow Ezekiel's initial vision of God's throne (chap. 1). Chaps. 4—5 report that he was ordered to undertake certain symbolic actions that predict the fate of Jerusalem, which had already been captured in 597 B.C. Ezekiel himself is with the captured exiles in Babylon. In the fifth year after that event (July 31, 593 B.C.; chap. 1:2) Ezekiel saw "the likeness of the glory of Yahweh" (1:28), fell prostrate, and experienced the audition with which our lesson begins.

It is characteristic of this book that the prophet is addressed as "son of man," human being, especially in contrast with the glory of God. Ezekiel's auditory experiences regularly (thirty-nine times) begin with this address, thereby reminding the priest-prophet who he is. Psalm 8 uses "son of man," first to emphasize God's care for a creature so small in comparison with the heavens, then to signal greatness in comparison with animals, birds, and fish. For Ezekiel, it is the smallness of the "son of man" (with respect to God) that is emphasized. To the auditory experience reported in v. 1 is added the "charismatic" one in v. 2—the Spirit, as a divine force, invades the priest and enables him to hear the commissions. The preexilic prophets seem to have distinguished themselves from the mantics whom the Spirit overcame (as in 1 Sam. 19:18–24), but this appears to have changed with the exilic and postexilic prophets, who claim the Spirit's empowerment (Isa. 42:1; 59:21; 61:1); no one emphasizes the Spirit-induced trances more than Ezekiel (see 3:12, 14; 8:3; 11:1).

Ezekiel is sent "to a nation of rebels" against God. Ezekiel is not sent to persuade them but to pronounce God's oracles (v. 4); he is not responsible for making them hear, but only for enunciating the God-given message. What matters is that people know that a word-bearing prophet has been among them (v. 5). Given such an assignment, Ezekiel needs to be fortified, for his life's work will entail suffering (vv. 6–7; see also 3:7–9). Yet in contrast with Paul (see today's Second Lesson), Ezekiel is given only the command "Do not be afraid of them."

Second Lesson: 2 Cor. 12:7-10. This lesson, unfortunately, breaks into the middle of the discussion; only enough of it is included to provide a brief setting for the word of the Lord in v. 9 and for the conclusion which Paul draws from it. Before the reading of it in worship, this pericope needs to be introduced with a few carefully crafted sentences which help the hearer understand the force of what Paul writes.

2 Corinthians 10—13 is commonly regarded as part of a letter which Paul wrote near the low point of his relation with the Corinthian church. Evidently, rival Christian teachers, whom Paul does not need to identify, arrived in Corinth and undermined Paul, who was at Ephesus

(11:3–6; note the sarcasm of v. 6). Apparently, they said Paul was a poor speaker (10:10; 11:6); his refusal to accept fees from his hearers, which would have been the customary thing to do, was held against him—a tacit admission on Paul's part that he had no right to be regarded as a bona fide teacher (11:7–9). These opponents (note the harsh language in 11:13–15) boasted of their Spirit-given powers. If our pericope is a clue, they also boasted of their ecstatic experiences. Paul's response often moves from the ironic to the sarcastic. He must defend his understanding of the gospel and his apostolic authorization as well; yet he realizes that if he tries to outscore them, he would be adopting the same mentality which he must overcome—boasting of his apostolic successes as a way of accrediting his message. So he boasts, but not of his prowess and achievements, but of his vulnerability (RSV reads "weakness," 11:30). His boasting is a parody of theirs (11:21–29). Whereas they seem to have explained their ecstatic experiences as the soul's momentary escape from the body in order to make contact with the divine Spirit, Paul says he too has had such experiences, but of course he does not know whether he was in or out of the body when these things happened (12:1–4).

Our passage begins with Paul's disclosure that he had so many revelations that God had to find a way to keep him humble—a thorn in the flesh was given to him. No one knows what this was; despite all sorts of guesses, there is no way to find out what it was. More important, Paul goes on to disclose his unanswered prayer that it be removed. In fact, the Lord revealed that his grace was perfected in weakness (v. 9)—*not* in the strength and success stories on which the opponents relied. Paul is content with vulnerability, hardship, and so forth, because this weakness makes it all the more clear that when faith in Christ arises, it is evoked by the gospel borne by a man like Paul, and it is faith in Christ and not in Paul. (He made the same point before: 1 Cor. 2:1–5.) There is no one-to-one correlation between the power of Christ and the power of Paul. Paul's acceptance of weakness is not a sign of masochism, nor of a weak ego, but of a strong ego under the cross (1 Cor. 1:18–25).

Gospel: Mark 6:1–6. (See Matt. 13:53–58.) Another story of Jesus' rejection at Nazareth is told by Luke, who uses it as the key signature of his account of Jesus' mission (Luke 4:16–30). In Mark, however, the story stands at the climax of a section which began at 3:13. Each of the three major sections of the first half of Mark begins with the theme of Jesus' call/commission of the disciples: (*a*) 1:16–20 begins 1:16—3:12; (*b*) 3:13–19 begins 3:13—6:6; (*c*) 6:7–13 begins 6:7—8:21. This section, in which our pericope stands, emphasizes the differentiation between those who are "with Jesus" and those who are not (3:21–22, 31–35; 4:10–12, 33–34). In our story the unbelief of Jesus' neighbors contrasts with the faith of Jairus and the hemorrhaging woman, which had just been told (5:21–43; see last Sunday's Gospel).

Mark does not tell us what Jesus taught (contrast Luke), nor does he say how the people knew about Jesus' deeds (v. 2). The story simply assumes that they knew the sort of stories about Jesus with which Mark has provided the reader. At v. 3 some manuscripts of Mark agree with Matthew, who changed "carpenter" to "the son of the carpenter" (Matt. 13:55). It has been suggested that calling Jesus "son of Mary" implies either that Joseph had been dead a long time or that it is a slight slur on Jesus, for Jewish men were known by their father (as "Simon, son of Jonah"). The brothers and sisters are mentioned naturally, without any hint that they were really cousins, half-brothers, or half-sisters. The folk of Nazareth could not square the words and works of Jesus with his identity; the readers, of course, know what the townspeople do not know—whence Jesus got "all this": from the endowment of the Spirit and from God's designating him as "Son" (1:9–11).

Jesus responds with a proverb (literally "parable"), which Matthew abbreviates (13:57) and which Luke gives in a different form (4:24). A noncanonical text containing sayings of Jesus (Oxyrhyncus Papyrus 1) has yet another variant: "Jesus says, 'a prophet is not acceptable in his own country, neither does a physician cure those who know him,' " which is virtually identical with the Gospel of Thomas, Logion 31. Similar proverbs are known from other sources in antiquity. The Marcan version is relentless: "except in his own country . . . kin . . . own house." Why? "Country" in v. 4 refers back to v. 1; "kin" may refer to 3:21 (RSV's "friends" could also be "his relatives"), and "own house" may refer to 3:31—thus binding the whole section together.

The conclusion of the story is less than clear. (*a*) On the one hand, Jesus was unable to perform a "mighty act"; on the other, he healed a few sick folk by touching them—he could be only a healer. (*b*) On the one hand, whoever applies the proverb to himself does not expect anything else; on the other, Jesus marveled at their "unfaith." The reader is invited to marvel also.

HOMILETICAL INTERPRETATION

First Lesson: Ezek. 2:1–7. The passage clearly was selected to complement the Gospel reading. There Jesus is described as being rejected by his countrymen; here there is given a rationale for Ezekiel's rejection.

Thus this passage may be used as background material for sermons centering on the Gospel pericope. But the passage may also stand alone as it provides some insights into the role of those called to speak for God in their day. However, if the latter is the decision, some care should be taken in drawing parallels. Ezekiel's call is described in terms of going to a rebellious people whose lives are set against God. Few ministers, even on their blackest Mondays, think so negatively about their mission to those in their congregation.

With these reservations, the following insights from the passage may be instructive either in relation to the Gospel lesson or for all called to speak God's Word.

Basic for the prophetic voice is faithfulness to the message; Ezekiel is sent to proclaim a word for his day. This idea, of course, cannot be responsibly developed without reference to chap. 1 and the understanding that message and mission grow out of Ezekiel's call and commitment. He, like all prophetic figures, was conscious that the message to be spoken was a message given. It was not the result of his intellectual ability or wisdom; it was from God. His mission was to be the medium of God's word. His responsibility was to deliver that message so that the word of God was being spoken in the midst of his people. One is reminded of a question that haunted Kierkegaard: "Have you uttered the definite question quite definitely?" This is the basic responsibility of the prophet.

But also, the prophet is not to be discouraged by the people's rejection of his message. His purpose is not to be accepted but to be faithful—certainly a word to be pondered by the occupants of the pulpit, especially when one is tempted to proclaim only what is palatable and popular with the congregation. We need to be freed from charting our mission sensitive only to popular response—not only freed from despondency in being rejected but also freed from elation at acceptance. The task is to speak the word; success or failure is left entirely to God.

Second Lesson: 2 Cor. 12:7–10. Paul has been caught up in a "bragging contest" with his opponents in Corinth and has cited spiritual experiences and sufferings to compete with their claims (11:12ff.). At the point where the reader becomes somewhat uneasy with Paul's boasting, there comes this "thorn in the flesh" to prick Paul's ego and to provide for us a significant insight into life. The insight is that God's power and grace frequently are manifested in human life not through strength but through weakness. The interpreter would be well advised to spare the congregation idle speculation about what the "thorn" is. It is enough to say that it is characterized by continual suffering which cannot be alleviated. Prayers for relief are unanswered; the weakness must be borne. There may be a temptation at this point for the interpreter to turn aside and deal with the subject of unanswered prayers, especially now with TV evangelists many times implying that "right" faith insures answered prayers—a kind of quid pro quo understanding of our relation to God. What then do we make of Paul's unrelieved agony?

However, the passage's main emphasis is in the consideration of strengths found in weakness, and in this there are several areas of consideration for the preacher. Consider how human weaknesses restore the sense of humility. Paul acknowledges, in a sense, that he was preening himself like a peacock until the thorn in the flesh tempered his self-esteem and restored perspective to his life. Many persons have felt in complete control of their lives, confident in themselves alone, until the sudden pain in the chest, the lump on the neck, or irrational anxiety has revealed their vulnerability and frailty. Consider how this human frailty may remind us of our complete reliance and dependence upon Christ. Self-confidence and self-reliance are strengths, but they also may be barriers to spiritual growth. Our need of something more than self is evident when suddenly our self-sufficiency is breached by human weakness. The chinks in our armor are often God's contact points in our lives. Thus it is in life that persons looking back on periods of human suffering difficult to be borne often see them in retrospect as times of spiritual growth, of ultimate dependence upon God. "For when I am weak, I am strong."

Gospel: Mark 6:1–6. The question of response to Jesus, a recurrent theme throughout Mark, is here again at the center of attention. Two weeks ago, in Mark 4:35–41, it was the response of the disciples' loyalty; they followed Jesus but with inadequate faith. Last week, in Mark 5:21–43, it was the surprising, unexpected response of the faith of Jairus and of the hemorrhaging woman. This week, the reading sets forth the unexpected response of rejection of Jesus by his neighbors. The genius of these pericopes is that we, in hearing them, become part of the story; we are called to respond.

Here the response to Jesus is immediate rejection. The disciples are willing to listen and to follow, but here Jesus is given little or no opportunity by his countrymen to convince or influence them. His fellow citizens listen to him teach; they reject him. The passage says nothing about the content of the teaching. Perhaps we are to assume that what he taught here was similar to his teaching reported throughout Mark: the announcement of the breaking in of the Kingdom of God in connection with his presence among them. However, his countrymen's peremptory rejection of him does not seem to rest on an analysis of the content of his teaching but simply on who he is: "Is not this the carpenter?" It was clear to them that God simply does not work his purposes out in the commonplace—in this person they had seen in their midst as a member of a family, called from play by his mother, working side by side with Joseph. These people of Nazareth, unable to accept God's working in Jesus, are precursors of all those who confront Jesus. The story tells, in its few verses, a basic struggle always swirling around the person of Jesus, taking theological form in the issue of Jesus' two natures, divine and human. The issue formulated in orthodoxy by the Council of Chalcedon in A.D. 451 is still before us whenever we face Jesus and ask the question, "Who then is this?"

Today, few have difficulty affirming Jesus' humanity. He represents for many a model of what true humanity is intended to be; he is the highest upward thrust of humanity toward God. But there is still a sticking point when confronted with what the NT affirms, that in Christ God thrust down into the midst of the human scene. When this is affirmed, once again the narrative is played, offense is taken, and he is rejected. And yet how profound a message and how necessary it is today—that our God, obscured in the vast reaches of our universe, is One who has revealed himself in the form of our humanity, so that we are inextricably with him and he with us.

The Eighth Sunday after Pentecost

Lutheran	Roman Catholic	Episcopal	Pres/UCC/Chr	Meth/COCU
Amos 7:10–15	Amos 7:12–15	Amos 7:7–15	Amos 7:12–17	Amos 7:7–17
Eph. 1:3–14	Eph. 1:3–14 or Eph. 1:3–10	Eph. 1:1–14	Eph. 1:3–10	Eph. 1:1–14
Mark 6:7–13	Mark 6:7–13	Mark 6:7–13	Mark 6:7–13	Mark 6:7–13

EXEGESIS

First Lesson: Amos 7:7–17. This lesson is part of a series of five visions which Amos experienced (7:1—8:3; 9:1). Even though they all have to do with coming doom, the fifth is quite different in form. The first two (locusts, 7:1–3; fire, 7:4–6) are characterized by Amos's interces-

sion on behalf of the nation, which results in God's turning away ("re-
penting") from the foreseen disaster. The other two (plumb line, 7:7–9;
basket of summer fruit, 8:1–3), however, lack this intercession, and,
accordingly, move relentlessly to the oracles of doom. These latter two
visions, reported in the first person, are separated from each other by a
narrative in the third person (7:1–17). Our lection combines the auto-
biographical report (7:7–9) with the biographical one (7:10–17). There
is a clear escalation from the former pair of visions (avertable doom) to
the latter pair (unavertable doom): the leaning wall must fall, and the
fruit must ripen and rot. When these visions, and the event of vv. 1–17,
occurred is not known; there is no reason to think that the literary
sequence reflects the historical sequence. Rather, material pertaining to
Amos's vocation has been assembled in a way that intensifies the experience of the reader. The third-person report is placed here because v. 9
mentions Jeroboam, who is mentioned also at the beginning of the next
unit (v. 10). Furthermore, by interrupting the series of vision reports
with this narrative, the editor heightens the dramatic effect of the whole
series.

The vision of the plumb line (note the repetition of the key word) is
interpreted by God: Israel will be devastated. The hilltop shrines ("high
places") shall be destroyed and the monarchy terminated by war.

V. 10 assumes that what Amos saw and heard he also proclaimed.
Nowhere else in the book do we read that he actually said what Amaziah
claims he said (v. 11). Is he putting words into Amos's mouth (that is, is
he "exegeting" Amos in a particular way)? Interestingly, whereas v. 9
juxtaposes doom for the shrines and doom for the monarchy, Amaziah
reported only the latter, and criticized Amos only for the former—which
he took to refer to the royal sanctuary (see 1 Kings 12:26–33). In short,
Amos had proclaimed God's word of doom for both the religious and the
political bulwark of Israel, but Amaziah reported it as Amos's word
about the king's doom and the nation's exile—thereby making Amos
subversive. Amaziah did not wait for the king to act.

Amos responded by appealing to the constraint under which he
spoke—God took him from his regular work. Amos was not a "professional prophet" but a "lay person" used by God. God's commission
overrides Amaziah's prohibition. The oracle actually pronounces doom
on the priesthood no less than on the monarchy. These terse lines, which
have reduced everything to essentials, embody a fundamental clash: the
God whose protection of the nation is celebrated at the shrines will turn
out to be its destroyer, not because God is unreliable, but because God is
reliable in zeal for justice. In light of the reliable uprightness of God,
epitomized by the plumb line, Israel has no future.

Second Lesson: Eph. 1:3–14. This remarkable passage—a single
sentence in Greek—weaves together fundamental themes of Paul's
theology and those of the author, who knew Paul's letters thoroughly.
(Those who, in contrast with the present writer, regard Paul as the
author must see Paul himself extending his thought beyond that of the
undisputed seven letters [Romans, 1 and 2 Corinthians, Galatians,
Philippians, 1 Thessalonians, Philemon].) Paul's own letters usually
move from the greeting to the paragraph of thanks; only 2 Corinthians
moves instead to a blessing (2 Cor. 1:2–3), and only Ephesians has first
the blessing and then the thanksgiving (1:15–23). Our paragraph moves
from phrases which refer to God the Father, to those which speak of the
Son (vv. 5–12), to those which speak of the Spirit. The relation among
the three is left as undefined as in the Apostolic Benediction (2 Cor.
13:14). Efforts to detect a hymnic structure have not succeeded; the
language, however, is formal and liturgical.

There are a number of distinctive themes here. One is "the heavenly
places" (v. 3). Even a cursory examination of 2:6; 3:10; and 6:12 will
show how interested the author is in the cosmic dimensions of the
Christ-event (see especially 1:22–23). The unification of the cosmos
under the lordship of Christ entails the evangelization of even the cosmic
powers (3:10). For the Christians to share in the blessings in the
"heavenly places" (see also 2:6) is to share in the triumph of Christ,
even though as earthlings they must yet battle hostile powers who are
not yet integrated into the cosmos (6:10–17). A second distinctive idea
can be found in v. 10, where the RSV translates *anakephalaiōsasthai* as
"unite." Literally it means "head-up," as in adding up a column of
figures. Here it means "integrate everything into Christ." Ephesians
lends itself readily to Christian triumphalism, especially since the
church is seen as Christ's body, in which the unity of all things is to be
manifest. A third distinctive accent appears in vv. 9–10—that to the
church has been revealed the purposes of God for the cosmos, the
"economy" of salvation (RSV reads "plan").

Throughout this intricate sentence are found a number of finite verbs
whose subject is God: God chose us (v. 4); God "begraced us" (v. 6;
RSV reads "grace which he freely bestowed"); God set forth his purposes in Christ (v. 9) and "sealed" us with the Spirit (v. 13). Christ is the
means by which God has done these things. They occurred not only
for human benefit but for "the praise of his glory" (triply emphasized:
vv. 6, 12, 14).

Gospel: Mark 6:7–13. Luke's version of this passage is found in
9:1–6. Matthew uses the passage in an expanded discourse on the

subject in chap. 10. In the first half of Mark, this is the third section which begins with the relation of Jesus to the disciples (see comment on last Sunday's Gospel); note how 6:7 carries out 3:13–15. The editorial work of Mark is fairly evident. Vv. 7 and 12–13 are the narrative framework, clearly from Mark. The charge to the disciples is actually double and diverse: the first (vv. 8–9) is an indirect quotation (which Matt. 10:9 and Luke 9:3 make into a direct quotation), and the second (using the introductory phrase which Matthew and Luke delete) gives a direct quotation. Each word has its own point; both were probably treasured, especially by wandering Christian preachers. Mark himself is more interested in the fact that the twelve did these things than in their experiences implied in vv. 8–14, for nothing more is said about them.

The Twelve are identified at 3:14–19. Why they were sent out by pairs (only according to Mark) is not said; probably, it reflects the Jewish view that two witnesses establish a point (Deut. 19:15). The Marcan summary in v. 12 adds that they preached repentance (there is nothing in the Greek text to correspond with "men" as RSV has it). No reason is given for the call to repentance. Mark assumes that the Twelve extended the mission of Jesus. Healing by anointing is known from the Jewish culture and is mentioned also in James 5:14. Mark probably also assumes that the practice, continued by early Christians, was traceable to Jesus' lifetime.

The charge in vv. 8–9 emphasizes the vulnerability of the emissaries. They are to move about as mendicants. In Mark the staff is the only protection permitted, whereas in Matt. 10:10 it is forbidden; in Mark sandals are commanded, whereas in Matthew they are forbidden. Matthew represents a more stringent tradition.

Vv. 10–11 are concerned not with the emissaries' own relation to the message but with their relation to their hearers. V. 10 requires that they not use their initial host's hospitality as a base while they find better quarters. V. 11 admonishes them to engage in a prophetic act—shake off the dust. The appearing of the Twelve with this word and deed has a juridical element in it—like posting a legal notice, it makes the hearers accountable. One is reminded of Ezek. 2:5.

HOMILETICAL INTERPRETATION

First Lesson: Amos 7:7–17. A first reading of the lessons for this Sunday indicates that this passage is intended to go with the Gospel in order to draw some parallels between the selection and rejection of Amos as spokesman for God to his people and the selection and rejection of the Twelve. While drawing such parallels may be a productive approach for the preacher, the intriguing element in this passage, in the immediate context of the American churches, is that it presents the two radically different understandings of the religious office typified by Amaziah and by Amos. The contrast between them may provide for both pew and pulpit some help in assessing that kind of modern, popular American Christianity which at times seems a mirror image of "nationalism with a halo."

Amaziah, a member of the corps of cultic priests attached to shrine and court, proclaimed the national religious party line of prosperity for the state and disaster for its enemies. As a cultic priest, his message was certainly based upon the religious conviction that the nation's existence was God's intention, that the nation was inviolable. Amaziah personifies state religion, a religion captive to national interest in the status quo, whose message is indistinguishable from that of the local chamber of commerce. On the other hand, Amos has no professional standing with the cultic priest; his only credentials are a sense of the authority of God calling him and compelling him to speak. One sees an illustration of his message (in v. 7–9) in the vision of the plumb line revealing the distortions in both the nation and its religion. Amos's message from God thus sets him over against nation and state religion and leads to his rejection from the shrine.

Late twentieth-century American Christianity has disturbing similarities to this scene of centuries ago. While we have no professional state prophets, we have been treated to a variety of national religious influences: a parade of preachers to the White House during the sixties, whose message was disturbingly an echo of national interests; in each election a resurrection of the concept of America's favored place in God's purposes; popular TV preachers, whose message is a strange blend of Americanism and Christianity. In this ancient scene, one confronts the question, What is the relation of religion to the state? One disarming insight is that consistent agreement and peace between the two is suspect. There is in both the First Lesson and the Gospel the assumption that God's word clearly spoken stands over against the human scene, and will at times be rejected.

Second Lesson: Eph. 1:3–14. This passage is a hymn of adoration. As John Mackay says in his book on Ephesians, *God's Order,* it is "comparable to the overture of an opera which contains the successive melodies that are to follow." The passage is a hymn interweaving themes or ideas affirming a God of cosmic purposes whose intentions to unite all humanity have been revealed in Christ. The question before the preacher is how to preach from an outburst of adoration that might better be set to music than to speech.

One needs to wait before such a passage to discover how its affirmation strikes the moment. There are two basic overarching and overlapping themes that arrest the attention and that speak to the modern dilemma. One is the affirmation of God's purposefulness, the other is God's intention for unity in the created order.

Affirmation of God's purposefulness catches one's attention in the context of the meaninglessness of life. A dominant philosophy in our age, felt though not articulated, is nihilism: life "is a tale told by an idiot, full of sound and fury, signifying nothing" (*Macbeth,* act V, sc. 5). Over against this concept of existence, this passage speaks of a purpose running throughout the universe. It presents the affirmation that we do not just happen to exist, but that our lives have their roots in God's purpose. This affirmation may be reflected upon under the following headings. (*a*) God has chosen us (the church) out of his love, before the foundation of the world. This is the concept of predestination (at times so overstated and misinterpreted) which runs throughout the NT, affirming God's purpose for the world. (*b*) God has chosen us in Christ to be his adopted children. This act of adoption is sealed in the cross. (*c*) God has chosen us and has revealed his purpose to us. The people of God are the means through which God is fulfilling his purpose of unity for the world.

The other theme which catches the attention is that of God's intention for unity in the created order. This catches our attention simply because of the divisiveness that marks our existence, running throughout the created order from the God-human rift to the barriers separating and alienating us from one another. God's intention in Christ through his church is to overcome this disunity. A sermon from this perspective would utilize some of the material mentioned earlier but would center upon God in Christ moving through redemption to heal the divisiveness between God and every aspect of the created order.

Gospel: Mark 6:7–13. The focal point of the passage is mission. The twelve disciples, often portrayed in Mark in a disparaging light because of their disbelief and inability to understand, now are presented in their importance to the gospel. They are sent out to carry on the mission of Jesus and so they become a paradigm for church and ministry. The homiletician should seek in the passage for those characteristics of ministry and mission that instruct the church's life in every age.

There is first the authority—Jesus. He is the one who chooses, commissions, and sends. These are quite ordinary people given extraordinary responsibility; their power comes not from their status in life but from the one who sends them. One hears, at this point, echoes of the

Amos lesson: "I am no prophet, nor a prophet's son . . . and the Lord said to me, 'Go prophesy to my people Israel.' "

There is the message. It is given in disarming brevity: "So they went out and preached that men should repent." The words suggest Jesus' proclamation of the breaking in of the kingdom (Mark 1:14–15). The disciples are to join in what Jesus has been doing: confronting the powers of evil, calling for a drastic change in humanity's relation to God, proclaiming the gospel. One must be aware that this message stands at the center; faithfulness to it is the determining factor in success or failure.

There is the opposition. Rejection is expected, assumed, as if the authenticity of the message naturally will result in it. The message places before the hearers a decision; their response is seen as a judgment upon them, not as a sign of failure of the messenger.

There is the urgency of the mission. The sparse accoutrements of the disciples denote their dependence upon God alone, but they also indicate what has been called their "eschatological haste." They lived with the awareness of the imminence of the breaking in of God's rule. Centuries have gone by, and the concept of living in the final days has faded, but the mission still carries this sense of urgency, the reality that one dare not neglect decision about life's ultimate meaning.

The Ninth Sunday after Pentecost

7/25

Lutheran	Roman Catholic	Episcopal	Pres/UCC/Chr	Meth/COCU
Jer. 23:1–6	Jer. 23:1–6	Isa. 57:14b–21	Jer. 23:1–6	Jer. 23:1–6
Eph. 2:13–22	Eph. 2:13–18	Eph. 2:11–22	Eph. 2:11–18	Eph. 2:11–22
Mark 6:30–34	Mark 6:30–34	Mark 6:30–44	Mark 6:30–34	Mark 6:30–44

EXEGESIS

First Lesson: Jer. 23:1–6. Our lection stands near the end of a section that extends from 22:10—23:8. This section is devoted to a series of oracles related to the kings of Judah, mentioned or implied in sequence, and concludes with the hope of restoration from exile. Our passage consists of two parts (vv. 1–4, 5–6); together with vv. 7–8 it looks

beyond the troubled present to the future. It is eschatological, but not in
an apocalyptic sense, for there is no hint of a rejuvenated earth following
universal catastrophe. This is not a future beyond the end of history but
an historical era.

The first oracle combines retribution and promise. The shepherds are
the rulers (perhaps not restricted to kings), whose policies have ruined
the nation. The metaphor of the shepherd for a ruler is found also in Jer.
22:22, and in Ezekiel 34. For a shepherd to scatter the flock is to do
exactly the opposite of what should be done. Jeremiah's and Ezekiel's
perception of political life doubtless diverged from that of the rulers,
who probably understood themselves to be acting responsibly. In v. 2,
the retribution is expressed by a wordplay: shepherds have not "at-
tended" to the sheep (provided for their well-being); therefore, God will
"attend" to punishment. V. 3 promises that the God who was at work in
the destruction (and scattering) of the nation will also reconstitute it; in
v. 4 God promises new rulers over a nation restored and prospering. The
juxtaposition of v. 2 ("*you* have scattered . . . and driven them away")
and v. 3 ("*I* have driven them") manifests the biblical paradox that
although God is the ultimate shaper of history, human actors are accountable for their deeds.

The second oracle promises the restoration of the Davidic dynasty,
not simply its continuation (as asserted in 2 Sam. 7:13). "Branch"
(*tsemach*) means "shoot," and so implies that it will appear after the tree
is cut down. The idea (but not the word) appears in Isa. 11:1; the theme
was taken up also in Jer. 33:15, Zech. 3:8; 6:12 (see also Ps. 132:17). This
king will rule with such rectitude that he will be called "Yahweh-is-our-
righteousness." The hope for a Davidic ruler who will be everything that
a king ought to be was one of the forms of the messianic hope found
also at Qumran and among Jewish Christians, some of whom regarded
Jesus as "Son of David." Already within the NT, there is ambivalence
about the adequacy of this designation (reflected in Mark 12:35–37;
Rom. 1:3–4).

Second Lesson: Eph. 2:11–22. For Ephesians, the unification of the
cosmos (see last Sunday's Second Lesson) has its counterpart in humanity—the cleavage between Gentiles and Jews is overcome in the church.
In this passage one metaphor gives way to another; yet the main line of
thought is clear: vv. 11–12 state the plight of the Gentiles (as seen through
Jewish eyes), vv. 13–18 state the christocentric resolution, and vv. 19–22
state the consequences. The resolution is neither a matter of getting
Jews to abandon Jewishness (apostasy) nor of making Gentiles into Jews
(proselytism), but rather of creating a new humanity in the church.

The characterization of the Gentiles does not simply endorse Jewish self-understanding, for v. 11 observes that theirs is a circumcision "done with hands," and that it is this group that calls Gentiles "uncircumcision." In the NT what is "made with hands" is always inferior to what is made "without hands" (that is, by God; see Mark 14:58; Acts 7:48; 17:24; Heb. 9:11, 24; 2 Cor. 5:1; Col. 2:11). The situation of the Gentile is seen in two ways: (*a*) nonparticipation or lack (without a messiah, lack of citizenship [RSV reads "alienated"] in the holy people, lack of hope and without God); (*b*) hostility between Jew and Gentile. Although these attitudes toward Gentiles were widespread, here the passage is governed by the christological interpretation of three elements in Isa. 57:19: (1) "Peace, peace," (2) "to the far and to the near," (3) "says the Lord." Each of these elements is taken up by our passage.

First (v. 13), in Christ the distant have been brought near, a theme explicated in vv. 19–22 (note the repetition of the terminology of distance/strangeness in vv. 12, 19). By faith in Christ, Gentiles are fellow citizens in the people of God. Second, Christ is the basis of peace because he destroyed the wall between Jew and Gentile and so created a new humanity by reconciling both to God. This is the most difficult part of the passage. Here it must suffice to identify problems. (*a*) Does the "dividing wall" allude to an actual part of the Jerusalem temple (the veil, or the wall separating the gentile area from that reserved for Jews), or does it refer to a cosmic "partition" which was broken by the Savior's descent to earth (see 4:9)? (*b*) How did Christ destroy, "in his flesh," the law? (*c*) Why was this destruction necessary for the creation of a new humanity (literally, "new man")? Third, "says the Lord" is taken to mean that Christ preached the same message ("peace") to the near and to the distant (v. 17). V. 18 relates the unification of humanity to another theme—common access to God (antidote to what is stated in v. 12) through the Spirit.

Vv. 20–22 are important to the ecclesiology of Ephesians. The church is built on the foundation stones, apostles and prophets, among whom Christ is the chief (not the same metaphor as 1 Cor. 3:11). Just as v. 18 combines Father, Son, and Spirit, so does v. 22 (see last Sunday's Second Lesson).

Gospel: Mark 6:30–44. (See Matt. 14:13–21; Luke 9:10–17.) Our lection begins by resuming the narrative from v. 13. Mark has no interest in Jesus' reaction to the disciples' success stories. The feeding story is one of the few found also in John (6:1–14), where it leads to a discourse on Jesus the heavenly bread. But also in Mark, the story has overtones of symbolic meaning: the Eucharist (v. 41); the tradition of divinely given bread (manna) in the wilderness; the superabundant food provided by Elisha (2 Kings 4:42–44); the twelve baskets hint of the twelve tribes (as Mark 8:1–10 hints of Gentiles with seven baskets); the shepherd who provides for his flock. Marvelous as the event is, Mark 8:14–21 shows that a miracle does not yet reveal who Jesus is.

V. 34 states Mark's reason why Jesus had compassion—the people were like shepherdless sheep (an allusion to Num. 27:17; see also Zech. 11:4). Matthew and Luke omit this detail but add that Jesus healed. For Mark, Jesus' compassionate response is his teaching. In their own way, the disciples are not without compassion. To their surprise, Jesus told them to feed the people. Their question (v. 37) expresses the hopelessness of the situation when seen in light of their resources. Undeterred, Jesus asks them to take inventory (the boy appears only in John and should not be imported here). In contrast with most miracle stories, nothing is said about the crowd's amazement. The crowd is passive throughout; it is Jesus who has the initiative.

This is not surprising, for we have a christological story laden with symbolic details and suggestions. Normally one should not allegorize miracle stories; in this case, however, to bring out the symbolic hints is to be faithful to the story and to Mark as well. Above all, one should not "rationalize" the story to mean that what occurred was a "miracle of sharing" (thereby also borrowing the boy from John). Rather, one should ponder what Mark says: Jesus is the one who does God's work—he feeds his flock like a shepherd (Isa. 40:11). Appropriately, the people (flock) sit on green grass (in the desert!). This is not an eschatological banquet (an apocalyptic theme) but a symbolization of the wondrous bread provided by the God-given shepherd in the wilderness, where the people of God are embarked on a new exodus.

HOMILETICAL INTERPRETATION

First Lesson: Jer. 23:1–6. Clearly the First Lesson complements the Gospel where Jesus has compassion on the multitude "because they were like sheep without a shepherd." The homiletician, however, must be careful not to draw too close parallels between the passages. The figure of the shepherd as ruler, leader, is a theme throughout the two testaments, but in Jeremiah the reference is to the political leader, while in Mark the reference may be to lack of ecclesiastical or religious leadership. The OT passage more relevant to the Marcan passage is certainly Ezekiel 34.

Jeremiah's oracle (vv. 1–4) is political, an attack against the last kings of Judah who have failed as shepherds, misgoverning the nation. The shepherd image was ideally suited to portray the able leader; the shepherd kept the flock together, prevented the sheep from being scattered, led and cared for them, and guarded them from all evil. (The words call to mind the shepherd image in Psalm 23.) The kings of Judah, to Jeremiah, had none of these qualities. God, therefore, would bring forth leaders to be true shepherds. It is understandable that, in this context, the compiler of Jeremiah places the oracle of the ideal king of Judah. In contrast to the weak rulers, there will come one who will be the ideal leader, executing justice and righteousness, saving the people.

But what does the modern preacher do with this ancient oracle having to do with weak rulers and a slowly dying nation millennia ago? Does it not speak of the universal hunger in the human heart for one to be leader, to care for and protect the people? Does it not also speak of those who desire to be leaders of the people, who put themselves forward as able to fulfill the hungers of the human heart? And does the passage not also suggest the failure of all leaders to fulfill the office of ideal leader, so that the hope never materializes? The passage then holds up before us in our modern political scene the ever-to-be-frustrated hope in political leaders.

Then against this realism the passage presents the ideal leader, the only possible fulfiller of the deepest longings of the human heart, the One sent from God. Here the message moves christologically toward the One who is to come, who has come, who will come, suggesting all others will ultimately fail us, and that only this One's help for us is sufficient.

Second Lesson: Eph. 2:11–22. As last Sunday's lesson from Ephesians emphasized the purpose of God in overcoming the great rifts in human existence to create unity, so this passage speaks concretely of the unifying power of God in Christ. The passage speaks of a particular barrier confronting the Christian faith, perhaps the greatest challenge it faced in its earlier years, the barrier between Jew and Gentile. Perhaps the greatest illustration of the barrier between the two groups can be seen in the architecture of the temple. The temple consisted of a series of courts, each one a little higher than the one before, with the sanctuary itself in the inmost part of the courts. First there was the court of the Gentiles, then the court of the women, then the court of the Israelites, then the court of the priests, and then the Holy Place itself. Only into the first of these courts could a Gentile come. Between it and the rest of the temple there was a wall or a screen of marble, and set into it at intervals were tablets which announced that a Gentile was not to proceed beyond that point. With this in mind, one can sense the power of the imagery used in this passage when describing what God has done in Christ, "for he is our peace, who has made us both one, and has broken down the

dividing wall of hostility" (v. 14). Christ overcomes barriers through his
life and death. This is the great purpose of the whole of his life, to destroy
the barrier between people and God and between one person and
another.

The imagery of the passage clearly goes beyond any concrete historical division to speak of God's purpose to breach all walls, all barriers
existing between races and nations, outsiders and insiders. All now di-
vided are to brought together in one "holy temple in the Lord" (v. 21).

Dividing walls of hostility—religious, political, ethnic—still stand
stark and somber in the human scene. To confess Jesus Christ is to affirm
from the vantage point of faith an end to division and hostility, separation and segregation. To proclaim Christ as Lord is to proclaim the
power of his love to destroy barriers in life and, at the same time, to
commit ourselves to that same purpose.

Gospel: Mark 6:30–44. This pericope should be seen in relation to
the previous passage in which Mark deals with the mission of the
Twelve. Here the mission is given further interpretation in Jesus' response and in the inadequacy of the disciples. As is true in so many
miracle stories, the value of the story is not on the surface, not on the
"how" of the miracle or on an attempt to explain it. The story provides a
window through which we see a wealth of messages: the compassion of
Jesus to the crowds, the response to their needs through teaching, and
the giving of bread. The focus of the passage is Jesus as the nourisher and
sustainer of the people.

Amid all the riches of the passage, the theme which arrests the
attention of the homiletician, conditioned perhaps by the First Lesson
for this week, is the emphasis upon the reaction of Jesus to the great
crowd of people: "He had compassion on them, because they were like
sheep without a shepherd." The imagery arrests the attention, suggesting a scattered, leaderless humanity without direction or purpose,
driven by hunger deeper than hunger for food, driven by desire for
something or someone to give meaning to life, to provide a center to hold
things together. How eternally modern is this image of humanity!

The great good news is that Jesus had "compassion" upon them. Our
English word does not capture the depth of emotion Jesus felt; he was
stirred to the depths of his being at the sight of the needs before him. He
looked upon the crowds not as we often do as inconvenient or a hin-
drance. They are his mission. He is moved always to minister to them.
The wonder of it is that Jesus' reaction to the human condition is God's
reaction; his compassion is God's compassion. Here is the basis for a
sermon dealing with the pastoral dimensions of the faith.